THE SECRET ART
OF LOBBYING

THE ESSENTIAL BUSINESS GUIDE TO
WINNING IN THE POLITICAL JUNGLE

THE
SECRET
ART
OF
LOBBYING

DARCY NICOLLE

\B^b\
Biteback Publishing

First published in Great Britain in 2019 by
Biteback Publishing Ltd
Westminster Tower
3 Albert Embankment
London SE1 7SP
Copyright © Darcy Nicolle 2019

ISBN 978-1-78590-505-6

10 9 8 7 6 5 4 3 2 1

A CIP catalogue record for this book is available from the British Library.

Set in Minion Pro

Printed and bound in Great Britain by
CPI Group (UK) Ltd, Croydon CR0 4YY

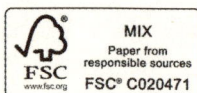

This book is dedicated to my much-missed grandfather, Sir Anthony Kershaw MC MP. He was a great international and UK politician who taught me that politics is all about people and inspired me to broaden my horizons.

CONTENTS

INTRODUCTION

How do you deal with political risk? What do you do about politicians making decisions that will inevitably fall on your business? Just sit there waiting for the inevitable? Grab an umbrella and hope the storm will pass? Or do you get out there and make your own political weather? This book is all about how you can get out there and win at the lobbying game.

The lobbying game is not the reserve for the privileged few with deep pockets, personal contacts and an encyclopaedic knowledge of politics. All that is needed is the confidence and the wherewithal to go out and make a compelling case, at the right time, to the right people.

Political decisions can earn your business money, save you money, open or close markets, or indeed destroy your reputation and business. Why leave this to chance by staying out in the cold? It sounds dramatic to say that 'if you are not in the corridors of power, your enemies will be', but even if you are lucky and they are not there lobbying against you, politicians will be making uninformed decisions that could impact you.

Lobbying is about dealing with a group of outsiders – politicians – that you cannot afford to ignore (much the same as dealing with investors, backers, legal complaints, the press or trade unions), regardless of whether your business is running a company, operating an association, or organising a charity or an interest group.

What does good lobbying look like? It is being asked if you agree with an imminent decision, having been the one who put it on the table in the first place.

So to become an influential player in the corridors of power, you must know what decisions are going to be made, who will be taking them and how to shape the debate and the decisions.

This sounds simple enough to say, but in fact all you need is to be systematic in your approach and positive in your attitude.

To fill you with confidence and thoroughly equip you for your journey in the corridors of power, this book covers the whole range of skills, capabilities and basic political knowledge you will need to win at lobbying – whether at international level, in a national capital or your local region, for both European and US organisations.

It will teach you what makes politicians tick, as well as

how to: plan your campaign and learn lessons from other successful campaigns; gather your arguments; leverage your influence; deal with political crises; be persuasive under pressure; and relentlessly focus on finding and using the levers of power and influence.

First off, though, when I use the term 'politicians', I do not just mean the ones you imagine holding grand parliamentary debates or attending international summits. 'Politicians' covers the whole gamut, from ministers and bureaucrats to mayors and agency officials – they are all making political decisions, whether they are elected or not.

Secondly, I will refer to 'political arenas' quite a lot – this is a shorthand expression to encompass all the political players that influence a specific political question. Covering not just the politicians, but all the other companies and industries, campaigners and pressure groups, journalists, academics and think tanks involved.

And lastly, 'political decisions' essentially come in two forms, as famously phrased by former US Defence Secretary Donald Rumsfeld: 'known unknowns' and 'unknown unknowns'. The first type is an undecided political decision that you can anticipate and plan for. The second is a political crisis that you cannot predict, but will probably trigger political decisions for which you can nevertheless prepare.

Lobbying is all about influencing political decisions before they are made. This book will show you how to get on the inside track, make your presence felt in the political arena and make politics work for you, so you are not the one left outside without an umbrella to protect you from political storms.

The first step on your journey to the corridors of power is to assess yourself and the political world – the politicians you will need to persuade to get real political leverage and the arena you will be operating in. Building on this foundation, this book will equip you with the tools and skills to go out and perfect the art of lobbying.

POLITICAL AWARENESS

In order to succeed in lobbying, you must first and foremost be politically aware. You need knowledge of the political landscape. What is your political profile? Are you aware of who and what politicians are about? Do you know which politicians you have to persuade? And are you aware of who else is in the political arena – your potential friends and allies – that you aim to be active in?

You can see this chapter as a political audit. This makes it sound a rather dry exercise, but it is the essential foundation stone you need to build on in aiming, planning and launching yourself into the political sphere. Without it, you are entering a strange new world, not only without a map, but with no idea where you are starting from and where you need to go.

KNOW YOURSELF

You run an organisation that makes products or offers services, and you want to keep your backers happy. That was easy – but now ask yourself, what are you, politically speaking? In order to answer this question, you need to put together your political profile.

Analysing your political profile – ten questions

1. Are my products and services regulated?
2. How do politicians view my products and services?
3. How do consumer groups, human rights groups and environmentalists view my products and services?
4. How does the press and social media view my products and services?
5. How do competitors view my products and services and how do I view theirs?
6. How do customers view my product and services?
7. Who and where are my suppliers?
8. Are the regulations suitable for my current products and services?
9. Are the regulations suitable for my future products and services?
10. Who and where are my employees, offices and factories?

The first question is, have you been honest? A bit cheeky, but have you given your answers a reality check?

If, for example, you run a car business and are a complete petrol head, you may be tempted to see your profile as a technically advanced company making wonderfully fast, smart machines that your customers love and the only thing holding you back are those meddling, know-nothing politicians who only listen to people who hate cars.

Tempting… but working from this viewpoint will not put you on the correct road to political savvy-ness.

However, this does illustrate the gap that needs to be bridged between how a typical business views its products and services and how many politicians see them (in this case, cars as dangerous, fuel-hungry and poisonous machines that clog up cities and make modern life a misery).

What I do hope is that you have had a look through these questions and will already be getting into the mind-set of seeing your business through the eyes of a politician. Knowing what makes them tick and how they may react is essential in order to make sense of what is going on and how to respond.

GETTING TO KNOW POLITICIANS

Are politicians Martians? No, but neither are they business-people, nor do they work in a marketplace. They live and operate in the political world, a place you have to get to know somewhat in order to succeed in it.

What makes them tick? The cynical answer is: power and influence and getting more of it. This may not always be the case, but they are hardly philosopher kings acting objectively and dispassionately for the common good. You have cut-throat competition, they have the greasy pole. They also have ideals, ideology and public opinion to worry about (as well as their egos…).

WHO ARE POLITICIANS?

The all-inclusive answer is – people making decisions on policies and laws. They come in many forms with different titles and roles, but the basic types in nearly all institutions, from the UN downwards to national and local level, are:

1. The Prime Minister and/or President.
2. Cabinet minister and mayor.
3. Junior ministers.
4. Senior civil servants.
5. Working officials.
6. Parliamentarians.
7. Advisors.
8. Government agency staff.

WHAT DO THEY RESPOND TO?

Each group needs to be approached distinctly and their power and influence will vary between political systems, but they all want to make well-received and hopefully good decisions.

If they are elected, they want to be in the public eye and ultimately re-elected. In Cabinet and committees they want to be seen as being well-informed and to be the one with the killer arguments. If they are unelected bureaucrats, they want ministers to recognise and approve their decisions, and although they are obviously less bothered about elections, they are still making political decisions.

Officials – civil servants and government agency staff – are a different breed from elected officials. They are administrators, organisers and implementers, and the subject specialists are more akin to academics. They vary a lot in personality like any group, but they are not gamblers, dealers, salespeople and entrepreneurs. If they were, they would be in the wrong place. They are ambitious, not to become millionaires, but to do well at their job, get promoted and grow their influence. They are values-driven and, in this respect, similar to elected politicians.

In politics, 80 per cent of the work is done by the working officials and ministry staff – in fact, make that 95 per cent! They are the people you will have to brief and try to get on side. The remaining 5 per cent is done by ministers, Cabinet ministers, Prime Ministers and Presidents – if you are looking to talk with them, you must have a real humdinger of a political problem to deal with.

Effective communication when you get up close and personal with politicians is dealt with later, but if you are talking to the top people, assume you have a maximum of ten minutes of real time with them. A half-hour meeting slot is easily compressed to twenty minutes as diaries are full and busy, and after introductions and niceties you will have only five to ten minutes in real time to make your point. You have to move sharpish to the meat of your case and your killer argument to allow time to talk to and convince the senior politician to care about your case and maybe agree to take action on your behalf.

The other essential fact you need to realise is that all these groups of ministries, parliaments and agencies lobby each other continuously – to compete in this arena you need to be good, as the competition is fierce just from the politicians, let alone the other players.

Your job is to feed politicians' needs and motivations – there is little point promoting ideas that are political suicide to politicians, or arguing with bureaucrats that they should stop doing their job and give up writing new laws.

If you can offer a vote-winning, eye-catching and practical solution to them, you are in an excellent position. Ideally, they will take up your ideas, claim them as their own and you win without actually fighting. But you still need to get yourself into the right position and talk with the right people, with the right arguments, at the right time to achieve this.

WHAT DO THEY KNOW ABOUT YOU?
Thinking back to your political profile, you must delve deeper and ask, what do the politicians actually know about you?

1. Do politicians know about my products, services and market?

2. Do politicians have a positive or negative view of my business?

3. Are they under pressure to act for or against me?

4. Do they know how many people are involved in my business and industry?

5. Do they know if I export, or want to export, my products and services?

6. Do they know that my business could be impacted by their decisions?

7. Are they only talking to other industry sectors or interest groups and ignoring me and my business sector?

8. Do they know how important my business and industry is?

You are the expert on your business, but it is a grave mistake to assume that politicians will know about your business or be aware of what is keeping you up at night.

You can be rightly paranoid that if you are not talking with politicians, your enemies are; however, the most common danger is politicians making uninformed decisions. Your job is to have a clear understanding of what politicians are trying to achieve and then make sure they are well-informed and at least make educated decisions when they act.

A telling example of an uninformed decision was made by a European Commission official many years ago that would ban the curing of fish without refrigeration. He was from the south of Italy and insisted that refrigeration was necessary to stop the fish rotting. Being from the warm south, he had no concept that you can cure mackerel in Scotland without refrigeration quite safely and produce kippers – a strong-tasting breakfast delicacy much loved in the UK.

The official did not have it in for kippers, he just did not know about them, nor the climatic conditions in Scotland. But the fact that the planned ban got so far in the decision-making process before being dropped should have been an embarrassment to the kipper industry and Scottish politicians, as they were obviously not briefing the officials who could have banned their produce.

HOW POLITICIANS MAKE DECISIONS

Senior politicians are keen to make broad-brush, sound bite-friendly decisions and statements, which might garner headlines and voter approval. It is rather like a chef presenting a great dish to diners – rapturous applause and no questions asked about the details of how it was actually cooked up are the order of the day. But real politics is all about the cooking process and the details. And, as in most restaurants, the actual preparation and cooking parts of politics are politely shielded from the customers.

Unless you are invited as a special customer into the political kitchen, how do you know or influence what is being prepared? The answer lies in the dynamics of group discussions and group decision-making.

There will be some cultural variations, but if you put more than half a dozen people into a room to make a decision, the majority will be silent – and it is usually the same dynamic in future meetings of the same group. So, if you want to influence a decision being discussed behind closed doors, speak to the people who actually talk and hold sway at the meeting. They are the political 'levers' that you to have to find and utilise.

LEVERS OF POWER

'Give me a lever and a place to stand and I will move the earth!' said Archimedes. And the same goes with lobbying – the key to solving any political problem is finding the correct political lever and then getting leverage to turn the decision-making your way.

A political lever is the influential decision maker(s) dealing with your issue – with the emphasis on influential. You are not trying to meet everyone who could possibly be involved. Without a laser-like focus on identifying levers and obtaining real leverage, you are wasting time and resources just talking to a lot of people and being active for activity's sake.

When you have a stable political system or a very local problem, the levers are usually pretty simple to identify by asking: Who is taking the decision? When are they due to make a decision? Where are they making the decision? As ever, political decisions are always made by people. However mechanical the process or however mechanical the people may seem, the human element is still central.

An example would be finalising an environmental report for a factory site. In the UK, you can find the official process on the Environment Agency website – a dry document setting out the formal procedure with submission dates, review periods and decision-making timings, but with no names of the people who are making those decisions. But of course there are people working inside and there will undoubtedly be someone deciding whose cases are on top of the pile and will be dealt with quickly. The challenge is to locate this person and persuade them to put your case on the top of the pile – then you have found your leverage point.

If your problem is something like getting planning permission for a new solar panel array on your factory roof, the levers are nearly all local. For example:

1. Who? The local council or commune officials, the mayor, councillors, the local parliamentarian(s) and possibly a central or regional government official.
2. When? You will find timings – the period between submission date and the official response, and so on – set out in local planning rules, which are usually found on the relevant website.
3. Where? The local regional authority.

But if you are faced by a new international requirement that will determine whether you can sell your product in Europe – for example, an environmental-rating standard – finding the who, when and where is trickier.

WHERE ARE THE LEVERS?

To illustrate how you may find the levers, we will stay with the example of environmental law, as this is an area of law where EU rules are particularly prevalent – similar to trade, competition, anti-trust and agricultural subsidies. Thus, the normal procedure for several decades has been as follows:

1. Who? The draft environmental law is probably driven by the 'north' – the Nordics, Germany, the Netherlands and the UK. The resistance usually comes from the 'south' or 'Club Med' countries – France, Spain and Italy. Central Europe is usually ambivalent or simply following Germany's lead.

2. When? There is an official plan and timetable on the websites of the different EU bodies, even if they are nearly always delayed.

3. Where? Meetings may be held in Brussels, but the policy decisions to support, resist or ignore the draft measure will be made in national capitals.

The key to finding out the influential leverage points here is to identify the core group of countries, often a minority, but who are vocal, consistent and present in driving the policy forward. Compared to other countries in the EU the Nordics are strongly in favour of stronger environmental laws and they make sure their officials are vocal, push a consistent message and actually turn up to European meetings.

You might be surprised about the emphasis on government representatives actually turning up to European meetings. But it is rare that all twenty-eight governments are around the table. Half or less is the norm. If your government officials or levers are not there in the meeting room, they are not going to move anything or influence anyone.

What usually happens is that in a room of like-minded government officials they will push for stronger and stronger environmental laws. This group-think bubble was often punctured by UK officials, who are typically well-briefed and tend to promote a pragmatic line. This often made the UK an influential player and a good leverage point to try to influence European meetings.

WHERE ARE THE LEVERS AFTER BREXIT?

Brexit will necessarily fundamentally alter the internal decision-making dynamics of the EU, and finding the right levers to aim at may get harder.

To illustrate this, if the UK decided to take a radical approach to plastic waste by banning plastic bags it could put the idea directly on the table and encourage the whole EU to do the same.

This would be a great opportunity if you are a maker of non-plastic bags.

You would go out and urge the UK government to leverage its influence to get the support of the Nordics, the Netherlands and Germany, and so gain enough support to push for an EU-wide ban on plastic bags. Simple.

In the post-Brexit future, you would still want the UK government to ban plastic bags as it sets a precedent, but you will have to find a new point(s) of leverage within the EU to get to your goal of an EU-wide ban on plastic bags. In this case, you will probably find it in Copenhagen, Stockholm or Berlin. Therefore, finding the levers of power will become more complex.

The certainties are that Germany and France will remain at the centre of things, wielding the most influence, and you can rely on the Nordics to remain active in environmental politics. But how the balance of decision-making will change, particularly in areas where the UK was traditionally an active supporter, is not clear. Such areas would be reforming the Common Agricultural Policy, promoting a single market for goods and services, trade liberalisation, deregulation, and science and research spending.

Smaller countries are already showing a new willingness to work together to push back against the French–German power axis. In the summer of 2017, while still flush from his victory in the presidential election, Emmanuel Macron failed to get his way when asking the EU to agree to a policy to curtail the ability of the Chinese to invest in Europe.

It was a classic anti-free trade policy push from France. President Macron got early support for his idea from the

German Chancellor who was happy to give him an early EU win. The UK – historically a champion of free trade that would have nixed this idea – was nowhere to be seen, absorbed as it was in internal political squabbles over Brexit.

What did happen was an unprecedented and successful alliance between Spain, the Baltic countries, the Nordics, Ireland, the Netherlands and Portugal joining together to say *non* to the idea.

France had wrongly assumed that, with the UK out of the game, all it had to do to push its agenda was to secure the political lever of Germany and the rest would follow. The French may have miscalculated, but the events revealed how new leverage points are emerging in the EU.

So even if you are the French President, you still have to find enough friends before getting your way. And as a private sector player, you will have to try even harder to find the right leverage points. You must find out who the influential decision makers are, when and where they are deciding on your issue, and leverage their influence – to do so, you must look in the political arena.

THE POLITICAL ARENA

To survive and thrive in the political fray, you need to know something about the political arena you are jumping into and, when in it, how to quickly identify who is important and influential and who could be potential allies – your potential leverage points. At the same time, you need to signal to others what you are about.

But what is a political arena? It is where the political players are and where the debate is happening. To put it in more illustrative terms, imagine an arena in Ancient Rome – not the type where Christians are being fed to the lions, but the forum outside the senate building, the busy crowd of citizens noisily milling and parading around, there to be seen, to speak out, to seek out their friends and assess their opponents.

The modern political arena is still very much the same – a people-centric space, broadened now by newspapers, news cameras, radio and social media. It is striking that in nearly every political debate, people still want to gather together – be it in conference halls, meeting rooms or on the street. People still want to be seen, to see who supports their issue, who opposes them and who are the leading voices.

When you are lobbying, your task is to thrive in that forum.

LOOK BEFORE YOU LEAP

Upon entering the arena for the first time, you will achieve more if you have prepared and have an idea of what the new forum is like. This sounds obvious, but some people do get this wrong and just charge in and make a total mess of things.

An American businessman turned up at a typical stakeholder meeting in Brussels – populated by the usual mix of national government officials, European Commission officials and a selected bunch of associations, business reps, and environment and consumer groups. It was an important event, as it was the first formal occasion for everyone involved to talk about new laws that would decide which chemicals could be used in manufacturing in Europe.

The meeting kicked off with the usual process of everyone introducing themselves and their key points in turn. When the American was given the floor, what did he do? He vociferously denounced the whole process. Firstly, he claimed he had been excluded from the political process (which he evidently had not been, as he was in the room); and secondly, he suggested that as the US did not have such chemical rules, there was no need for Europe to have rules either – which was not a great point to make to a room full of European bureaucrats. Unsurprisingly, his views went down like a lead balloon. But what was astonishing was that he thought he had made the killer argument. He was never seen again.

In a similar vein, a senior German businessman went to the European Parliament and turned up for a small discussion meeting with the chairman of one of the Parliament's committees – an important player. The German grabbed the floor and gave an uninterrupted twenty-minute rant about why the European Parliament in general, and the committee in particular, should immediately stop legislating on laws that could impact his industry. The chairman, a fellow German, was pretty thick-skinned and managed to smile and nod during this tirade, before politely leaving the meeting without comment. Apparently the businessman felt good afterwards and thought that his comments had really struck home.

Both these men had failed to survive the political arena. They did not know or learn about the forum they had got into and, once there, their arguments were not only irrelevant, but insulting. They were the proverbial bulls in the china shop and I still remain amazed that in both cases the men were convinced they had done a great lobbying job.

WHO REALLY MATTERS TO ME?

After getting to know a bit about the political arena you are entering, once there you should look to see where your potential leverage points and allies are.

Start by identifying the most powerful players. These are probably governments, specific ministries or ministry departments, parliamentarians, specific committees and political parties. Then move on to other political players in the room: industry associations and companies; trade unions; the media and specialised press; activists from non-governmental organisations (NGOs); academic institutes and think tanks; regulatory agencies and advisory bodies – in UK jargon, quasi-autonomous non-governmental organisations (quangos); and political consultants. A bit of a list, but you name a political arena and you'll come across nearly all these 'players'.

Once you have identified the players, you need to assess who are the real influencers who can help you. There is no point in spending a lot of time talking to people in the arena who have little influence on what you need to achieve.

Essentially, the bigger your political aim, the larger your political arena will be and the more people and groups you will have to get on your side. But to reach out to other groups is not always an easy thing to do. Before taking a closer look at the groups you find in a political arena, it is instructive to look at two areas that cause particular problems that can face companies – collaborating with activist groups and working with new decision makers.

WORKING WITH ACTIVISTS

The strength of activist or campaign groups is that they are seen in the political arena as representing the interests of private citizens (voters), unlike companies who work for the interests of their shareholders (profit). They are often viewed as opposing forces with competing agendas and, yes, they do spend a lot of energy attacking each other. But if they can work together, despite their differences, they can be a powerful political combination.

If you are looking to reach out to an activist group, you need to have a dispassionate look at yourself, as well as them – identify the cultural differences and ensure that you have a clear idea of the mutual benefits that collaboration could offer to both sides.

You are in business, you want to be successful; they are idealists and also want to be successful. You may have difficulties understanding where idealists are coming from and they may well fundamentally distrust your economic imperatives. In some areas there may not be any mutual interests, but there is usually one there if you look for it.

Take pedestrian safety, for example, which was the cause of a bitter row between activist groups and the car industry. There did not seem to be any mutual ground between the activists hotly accusing the industry of not caring about protecting pedestrians and the carmakers' outraged response that the activists' demands were impractical as they knew nothing about making cars. Despite this, they did eventually find a mutual interest, as both wanted better-designed crash tests and, working together, they successfully persuaded the politicians to change the official rules. This is an example of a successful combination of technical expertise from industry and democratic oomph from activists.

Finding a way towards mutual help requires patience and allowances from both sides. I found it best to get the profit thing out of the way immediately by saying, 'Of course I am out to grow my business. And even if I am from business, it does not mean I do not support your values and your drive to change society for the good.' This is much better than trying to ignore the elephant in the room: that you are just out to make money. I am not saying that it is easy, or that it will be a smooth road, but you need to start out by being positive and frank.

I have painted a pretty black and white picture of the business and the NGO world. If you are lucky, the values and outlook of your company will be not too far apart from that of a business-friendly NGO, and both of you will agree quickly to join forces to win the political game. That would be ideal.

NEW DECISION MAKERS

What happens when you find that a different ministry department from the usual has taken it upon themselves to make rules about your business? This happened in three cases with the European Commission when it started to make rules on: carbon dioxide emissions from cars; whether lead and mercury could be used in electronic equipment; and which chemicals could be used in making products. Traditionally, such rules for products would have been made by the industry department of the European Commission and signed off by industry ministers, rather than the environment ministers who did so in these instances.

In each case, the initial reaction of industry was an outraged 'Who do they think they are!' and 'They know nothing about our business!', as well as bemoaning that environment ministers 'hate industry and only talk to environmentalists'.

In each case, the respective industries did manage to get the environment department to share some of its power with the industry department and ministers. However, this was only a limited victory, as the industry failed to realise that the political balance of their arena had changed. Now it was the environment departments and environment ministers who held the whip hand and no longer the industry ministries.

The industry took too long to adjust to this new reality and did not start talking constructively with the new decision makers. During their adjustment period, the politics was needlessly combative and the industry lost many of its arguments. But, more damagingly, the new rules still came in and were ill-designed. The new politicians did not know enough about the practicalities of the sectors and technologies they were dealing with, because the industry had not been talking with them. A bad lobbying mistake.

This is an example of how the dynamics of a political arena change when new decision makers are involved, but the dynamics also shift when new activists or new industry competitors arrive. Just think of the advent of budget airlines in air transport and Uber in urban transport that have radically changed the political landscape. At first the incumbents resist the newcomers, but instead they should be changing their attitudes and adjusting to the new state of play.

Political arenas are an ever-changing tableau of players and in order to thrive you need to be flexible and able to react. Just like in the forum in Ancient Rome, you can never be quite sure who will turn up.

You are out to make your mark in the crowd, see who is important, find allies and assess opponents. Prepare before you leap into the arena and be prepared to work with new partners. Above all, be flexible, and adapt and react to the changing dynamics of your political arena.

Now you need to enter the political fray and you need a plan.

PLANNING YOUR CAMPAIGN

Awell-planned and well-resourced campaign will maximise your chances of success. In this chapter we look
at: the basic planning steps; choosing sensible options and
discarding unwise options, such as trying to buy influence;
targeting your efforts at the correct political layers; how to
get best value from external help; and the need for the whole
project to be underpinned by good intelligence.

STRATEGY AND TACTICS

The difference between strategy and tactics is that with a
strategy you are planning to win a war and with tactics you
are planning to win a battle. Of course, you can win a war

with one battle, but that should not change the mind-set with which you define your strategy.

One way to look at it is that you look forwards to the final goal when setting a strategy and then reason backwards to set your tactical goals.

WHAT IS THE GOAL?

If you have written down your political goal and it is more than a couple of lines long, think it through again; it should be short and sweet.

For example, the goal in business is to keep your shareholders happy, usually by earning more by selling more products. Why will people buy more of your products? Your strategy will look to leveraging factors like your pricing, quality and brand reputation to change or influence market behaviour.

It is similar in politics when you are trying to shape decisions, or indeed change the terms of the debate in your favour. Your goal is still to earn more, but your strategy is to leverage the strengths of your reputation – to be seen as 'the pioneer', 'the experts', 'the consumers' champion', 'the responsible investor', 'the enabler of healthy living'. Achieving this strategic positioning translates into greater political influence and increased sales. The link to sales and business is vital – if you are not working towards a business goal, what is the point of the political campaign?

A great example of how to change the terms of a debate by successfully focusing on a strategic goal came in the field of animal welfare. Rules were being put into place in the European Parliament to stop pharmaceutical drugs from entering the food chain – a clear and relatively uncontroversial measure until it turned out that the policy could prevent the treatment of pet animals like horses and rabbits (as they too could become part of the food chain).

This concern was going to be brushed to one side as a minor issue, but a lobby – a coalition of animal charities and the vet medicine industry – sprung up to defend the interests of pets, which quickly got the support of European parliamentarians. The terms of a dry debate about food chain safety had been radically transformed into a much more emotional question of pet welfare. A compromise had to be found, one that was good for both pets and the pharmaceutical industry. It was a brilliant strategy by the pet lobby.

However, focusing on a strategic goal is not necessarily easy. Regulatory attacks, political complexity, controversy and confusion can all act to obscure the essential purpose of why you are walking around the corridors of power. It is essential that if you have a government relations team or consultant working for you, they have a clear idea of your goal and strategy.

All too often one meets businesspeople and their representatives who say they are busily doing 'great politics' and have the photos to prove it, but who then complain that they do not really have a clear idea of the company's strategic goals. In essence, they are being paid to rush around the corridors of power, confusing activity for the achievement of a goal.

Similarly, too many association meetings grind to a standstill with no agreed actions, as no plan has been agreed upon, the lack of which confuses the logic of decisions and undermines focused action.

The strategic goal may be short on words, but it will be a powerful and essential catalyst for directed action.

Goal-setting gives you and your team focus, and sense and purpose to your actions.

WHERE ARE WE?

Once you have set your strategic goal, the next step is to travel backwards and assess where you are. This has to be a dispassionate exercise to objectively assess the reality of your situation.

- Are political arguments and trends against you?
- Are you in a period of austerity and cutbacks, but need to ask for public funding?
- Is politics dominated by free-marketeers, but you want government intervention into the market?
- Are your export markets difficult to enter and operate in?
- Is there a law preventing you from selling your product?
- Do you need a new law to sell your product?
- Could a new policy stop you selling your product?

- Are politicians aware of, or in fear of, your technology or new service?
- Have your competitors sewn up the market and so prevented your entry?
- Are your competitors unfairly subsidised?
- Are you influential enough to achieve your goal?

These are the types of questions you need to ask yourself in order to build up an accurate political picture of your situation and avoid the pitfall of confirmation bias by only seeing things that confirm your views. Look at what you think is the most biased report or political comment about your product or sector – you will probably not like it, but it is a good reflection of where you are politically speaking.

All plans need a reality check, so do not miss out this stage.

WHAT'S STOPPING US?

The next step is to identify the political roadblocks – the critical decision-making points – that you will have to face and battle through or sidestep to get to your goal.

The potential list of decision points can look daunting when faced with a complex political problem, so simplify your task by starting with the 'must haves' – probably the final decision-making points (for example, a Parliament having to give it a positive vote, or a minister having to sign off on it).

Then assess what has to take place before these key decisions can happen (for example, a parliamentary committee has to approve it, or the minister's advisors have to support the decision).

Repeat the process, identifying the next layer of decision-making or influence-forming. To continue to use our example, this could be that a certain number of parliamentarians will have to be energised to take action, or that the ministry has to be pressured into taking action by industry stakeholders.

You will end up with a hierarchy of targets to aim for in order to progress towards your goal and will probably have moved on to thinking about what actions you could take, such as how to contact certain parliamentarians and get the support of industry stakeholders to pressurise the ministry.

WHAT ARE OUR OPTIONS?

Focusing on your targets, what are you going to do? What tactics are you going to employ? How are you going to influence the relevant decision makers?

Focus and relevance are crucial. To put it in military terms, the best approach is accurate sniper fire. Massed artillery – showering parliamentarians with leaflets, or trying to see everybody – does not work.

Irrelevant 'nice to have' options – like getting coverage in press which has nothing to do with the parliamentary committee or spending time and energy arranging a visit by a friendly minister who has no influence on your issue – have to be stripped away.

This may sound obvious, but I have seen many expensive campaigns launched at the European Parliament that were full of sound and fury, but as the parliamentarians did not actually have the power to take action on the campaign issue, they could only generate hot air and it signified nothing politically. But it cost a lot…

Make sure your options are sensible. A good test is: would you be happy to see it in the press in the morning? An example of an option that would fail this test is the use of a pseudo-politician whose strings you could pull like a puppet to present your case.

There is actually an old nineteenth-century word for this type of politician, the wonderful sounding 'quockerwodger', derived from the name for a marionette puppet. I have come across this tactic once regarding a fake ambassador at an international meeting. When he started speaking something just seemed off, as all his lines seemed to come straight from a corporate hymn sheet. We quickly found out that not only was he not from the country he supposedly represented, but he was in fact a lawyer from Washington DC. Once his cover was blown, he lost all credibility and retreated rapidly from the scene, leaving a political campaign in tatters behind him. This was not a sensible tactic and one that could have only been born from desperation. It would have definitely failed the 'do you want to see this in the papers' test if the planners had stopped to think through their plan.

Another risky tactic is buying influence – probably what a lot of people think a book about lobbying would be all about – but I will tackle this later.

Instead, the sensible options are: meet key decision makers; plan CEO interviews on site with news crews; join a government-sponsored trade mission; prepare communication materials; identify conferences and hearings that you could speak at; join formal stakeholder groups; submit comments to government consultation exercises; speak at parliamentary committee hearings; join an association; get an association to act and have a social media presence; reach out to NGOs and other external stakeholders; commission research; brief the media; attend PR events; seek out celebrity endorsement and support; and conduct publicity stunts.

All these options have their role in influencing the terms of the political debate in your favour. Use the ones that are most suited to your target, purpose and means.

Means, in terms of time and money, are always limited. However, these limitations often spur creative thinking, as you have to work harder to maximise your resources. When assessing how to change UK government policy on granting pensions to its army veterans from Nepal (known as Gurkhas), the goal of taking on the UK Department of Defence and the UK government must have been daunting for the

Gurkhas – truly a David versus Goliath situation. Their option of getting the active and energetic support of the famous British actress Joanna Lumley was a stroke of genius. They got their issue into the political and public eye, twisted the arm of government and won, despite all the odds being heavily stacked against them.

SETTING OUT TO WIN

The final stage in the process is converting your chosen options into actions.

Firstly, you must formulate a summary of the goal you want to achieve and your key arguments. This document is initially aimed at cementing internal agreement with everybody involved in the effort and endorsing it. Then it can be used as the basis for all external communication during the campaign. The shorter it is the better.

Once you get going on your campaign, setting priorities and agreeing to have regular reviews are important, as this helps to retain momentum. Success breeds success – not only does your team see the success, but so do politicians and other 'stakeholders' in your political arena. Momentum is a powerful motivator and dynamo for a winning campaign. You can help this process along by first identifying small victories to aim at that the team can recognise, celebrate and build on.

When you are setting priorities, avoid trying to look at the whole mountain you have to climb. Focus on what needs to be done today and can be achieved in the short term. If you have a complex political issue, it is useful to define 'short term' as the next ninety days, but no longer. This keeps you focused on your next steps and prevents you from being overawed by the mountain. Short time periods for action and reviews provide the drum beat for a campaign, keeping the momentum going and giving you flexibility.

If you have never done anything political before, the formal legislative process can look complex. Text books love complicated flow charts that confuse more than they clarify. So keep things simple and only focus on the next political stage – for example, a committee hearing. Once you are close to completing that stage, then think and plan for the next.

When you are reviewing your campaign, the goal should remain unchanged and the focus should be on assessing where you are and what your next actions are. Have you made an impact and moved things forward? If you have not, reconsider the options you have chosen. Are they still good ones? Should other avenues be explored? Even if things are going well, review the chosen options and confirm that you still want to pursue them. It is in the natural order of things that plans do not survive contact with the enemy, so you need to be flexible and to react to changing political circumstances.

Always agree on actions at each review. Self-congratulatory reviews of the past, or communal moaning sessions about the unfairness of politics will get you nowhere. Keep looking forward to your next goal. This gives your campaign activity discipline and focus.

The simple planning process outlined above is best known as the GROW model and is a useful technique for going step by step through your:

- Goal.
- Reality.
- Obstacles and options.
- Way forward.

Of course, there are other planning techniques you can use, but I find this one is the most simple and logical.

It can be frustrating if your company is in the middle of a political campaign that might have a material impact on your business and you are responsible for making financial plans for the future, as the outcome of political battles can be uncertain. But a robust, regularly reviewed plan with a clear strategic goal will give you a time schedule and a balance of probabilities to work with.

CAUTIONARY NOTES

On a cautionary note, keep your plans secret. Plans for political influence appear Machiavellian because they are. A plan strips away the personalities and perceived values of politics and politicians. They look suspicious, inhuman and calculating.

People may know that many forces must be trying to sway

the political process, but they would much prefer to think that politicians are the only ones involved and that they are above influence. An idealised and mistaken view, but comforting nevertheless. But seeing an actual plan for political influence is irresistible to journalists. As Bismarck allegedly put it, 'Laws are like sausages, it's better not to see them being made.'

Just getting data on how many times a company has met with or emailed a politician can make the front pages: 'Industry met minister ten times and sent 100 emails.' Obviously something suspicious is going on. This kind of data is usually available using public information laws, so be prepared for it to become public – and be parsimonious in your emailing.

If you are regularly meeting politicians you may have to register as a lobbyist. This usually involves stating your company's name, its interests and maybe even what issues you are active on, together with the money spent on lobbying and the numbers of company people involved.

These details are published on official websites and gather dust until they are inspected by journalists looking for a story, or NGOs wanting to kick up a fuss. You can also use them as a guide to see if your rivals are meeting politicians. However, they do of course lack qualitative data to show how influential a lobby actually is.

BUYING POLITICAL INFLUENCE

Buying political favours and influence is tempting as a political shortcut – people are greedy and there will always be takers.

It is a favourite ploy by the media to disguise themselves and offer bribes to politicians to see who takes the bait, and many do get hooked into a political media scandal. This generates good headlines, with newspapers able to show that democracy is being undermined by shadowy lobbyists and villainous middlemen. It makes for a sensational story and bribery no doubt exists to some extent in nearly all political systems.

Money is always involved in politics, as parties and election campaigns do not fund themselves.

There is a sliding scale for private money entering the political system: at the top is an outright bribe to a politician or his 'favourite charity', which is clearly illegal; and at the bottom there is someone paying their party membership fees, which is clearly legal and indeed encouraged. In between, you have money donated for election campaigns, which is legal and encouraged in the US, legal but tightly controlled in the UK, but illegal in some other countries where parties rely on public funding. Then you have a country like Germany where private money goes in obliquely via think tanks that support specific parties – such donations are an important door-opener in the German system.

Politicians are elected by the electorate, but the modern politician is also a member of a party. Do party members, who pay for the party electoral campaigns and conferences, have the right to expect the politicians to follow their wishes? And if they are a major contributor, should they have a commensurately higher influence on party policy? Is this money just a big bribe dressed up as a party donation? How does a business fit in? Should a business put money into the party system and expect a return? Should the head of a business donate money ostensibly as a private citizen and expect a result – at least privileged access to senior politicians? Is hiring a politician as a board member or special advisor just another way to bribe a politician? How should the public react to headlines like, 'Large donor calls for the Prime Minister to change course'? With suspicion, I think – why should a wealthy person be able to play politics just because they have given a lot of money to a political party? It hardly fits well with the 'one man, one vote' view of democracy.

So many questions are raised by mixing private money and the political system, and there are grey areas despite laws trying to regulate it. US law goes into a lot of detail on what constitutes corruption – banning practically everything involving giving money to US or foreign politicians and officials, all the way down to not being able to offer a cup of coffee to an official. But, conversely, large corporate and individual donations to US election campaigns are not a problem. What do these donations 'buy' for the donors?

Transparency reporting requirements – for example, ministers and MEPs declaring who they have received gifts from – and freedom of information requests for how many invitations to dinner and art exhibitions an agency has accepted can shine an uncomfortable light on the donors.

When an ex-foreign minister in the UK declares that he received money from a foreign government or used a private plane to go on holiday, what impression does it give about the donors when it is reported in the media? Not a good one.

When an agency declares that it has received and accepted dozens of invitations for dinners and gala events from the industry it is regulating, it becomes increasingly hard for the agency to claim that it is neutral in its dealings. It therefore loses out in the public and media debate, to the detriment of itself and ultimately the industry it is regulating.

From the point of view of solving a political problem for your company, buying your way to a solution is a poor investment. It will probably lead to tears. It will never look good in the papers: when it comes out, your reputation is ruined; and if has not come out yet, it is the sword of Damocles hanging over your business and your reputation.

All in all, donating significant money to a political party may result in gratitude, recognition, door-opening and honours, or it may land you in disgrace – possibly both. There is no getting around the fact that private money is looked at with suspicion by the general public, even if it is needed to keep the political wheels turning in modern democracies.

However, once you have made your choices in the strategic planning stage, you must move towards taking action; effective lobbying depends on targeting the right political levers at the right time.

WHO TO SPEAK TO AND WHEN?

WHICH POLITICIANS DO I NEED TO SPEAK TO?

The machinery and mechanics of politics is obscure to outsiders – it is a big cloud made up of different ministers, officials, parliamentarians, UN agencies, EU politicians, Eurocrats, mayors, local communes and agencies. Out of this cloud, you hear thunder and hope to avoid the lightning bolts.

All the pieces do in fact fit together, seamlessly sometimes and messily in others – it depends on how complicated your issues are as to how many parts you'll have to deal with. For example, when working on a government grant for a factory, we had only one parliamentarian and one national ministry to work with. But launching a ground-breaking technology for supermarkets meant talking with politicians from nine different countries and the European Commission, while a project for a wind turbine failed because one parliamentarian was overlooked.

To make sure you are mapping out and talking to the right politicians at the right time, it is helpful to have a rough idea of how the political system works and how rules emerge.

MAPPING THE POLITICIANS

To simplify the political world, it is easier to split it into layers, with local politicians forming the bottom layer and international organisations like the United Nations at the top. In between are the European, national and regional levels.

The first task is to have a clear idea of which layer(s) your problem should fall into. I say 'should', as problems can jump around. If you have a local planning permission issue, it is clearly chiefly a local matter, but if you get no joy, you could take your case to the next layer up – the minister or regional government. Alternatively, if your product is being banned from a country market – which is a national issue – you could take the problem up to the EU level and find yourself speaking to the European Commission, or a European parliamentarian.

The humble fridge is a fine example of something that appears in all the layers. Fridges used to have refrigerants inside them that damaged the ozone layer. The ozone layer is dealt with at the international level by the Montreal Protocol (part of the United Nations Environment Programme (UNEP)) which covers over 190 countries. The law to ban these fridges was made by the EU, but enforced by national governments and finally policed by regional and local authorities. If you were really into fridges, you would have had to map out all the layers from top to bottom to make sure you were talking with the right people.

As far as timing is concerned, the further up you go, the longer things take. Four years is a short time to decide something in UN reckoning. Meanwhile, EU decisions take about eighteen months, and national and local decisions usually take less than a year.

If you are reading this and are facing a live political issue, here is a quick rundown of the political layers and how they interact.

International

The international layer is populated by an alphabet soup of organisations, including UNEP, ICAO, IMO, ITU, WCO, UNECE and UNFCCC (which deal with the environment, aerospace, maritime, telecoms, customs, transport and climate change respectively).

Their interaction with the European layer can be a bit messy, as European nations are members of the UN organisations but the EU, as a non-nation, is not. Therefore, sometimes the international rules are enacted nationally and sometimes by the EU, for example international food transport and danger signs on large trucks.

European

At the European layer, some laws are directly enacted without deviation at national level (known as regulations), some can be tailored within limits in national law (known as directives) and some are advisory, giving more latitude in how they appear in national law (known as decisions).

The average time it takes to make a law from start to finish is about three years – two years in the Commission and national expert stage, and one year to get through the political phase. The more controversial the issue, the longer it takes to go through the Brussels law-making machine.

European agencies

There is a level of simplicity that comes with EU agencies, which are single entities that set Europe-wide rules for things like aerospace safety, patents, medicines and chemicals. Surely everybody should be happy all round, then? Unfortunately not, as the agencies are still relatively immature. A good example was the European Chemical Agency assessing what chemicals could be used in aerospace production processes – a new area for them. The young agency lacked a deep pool of experts to call on, so one session saw the strange sight of an animal vet working for the agency surrounded by aerospace engineers trying to explain the corrosion performance of aero parts. Needless to say the session ended in mutual bafflement.

National

For most commercially relevant rules, the national level is mainly about putting EU-derived laws into place. But national officials and ministers are also part of the process at EU level – in fact, they are the most important decision makers. The reality is that there is no clear cut-off in terms of law making between the European and national layers – they mingle.

Regional and local

At local or regional level, you have mayors and councils, as well as the regional offices of environment agencies. They look at local issues, such as planning and permitting, local waste, and sometimes energy generation and distribution (as in the case of Germany).

Most of the time the layers mesh well, but sometimes they do not. If you are moving waste around, you have to deal with a nightmarish mix of local, national, European and international rules that can conflict. Your local laws may allow you to load up your waste on a truck, but there are no guarantees that the local rules at the destination point will allow you to unload.

HOW TO TIME YOUR LOBBYING

If you are facing a problematic law, whether European or national, the whole process can be broken down to six stages. Lobbying happens before and during all of the phases, but it gets harder each time to influence the shape of the legislation, which becomes more concrete the further down the process you go. It is therefore key to start lobbying as early as possible. On one European issue, we started in earnest two years before the first political text was seen.

The six stages are as follows:

1. The proposal – an initial decision to go ahead and do something, either made by a minister,* assembly or

---

* I have used 'minister' as shorthand for any top decision maker in a system – this can vary from a head of government for a UN decision, governments and European Parliament jointly for single market legislation, or a government or mayor at national and local levels.

Parliament, or triggered automatically by a review date in an existing law.

2. The study – officials conduct a study quantifying and assessing the problem, with suggestions on possible law-making. External consultation with stakeholders may happen.

3. The Green Paper – officials assess the study and decide on possible actions, which is summarised in a Green Paper to show to the minister and ask for outside opinions.*

4. The White Paper – officials draw up a policy document containing the rationale for the policy and draft legislation. The policy is firmer now and external consultation with stakeholders may happen.

5. The bill – a minister approves the draft legislation and the bill goes out to the Parliament for their debate and approval.

6. The act – the legislation is approved by the minister and the act enters the law books.

Not featured in this outline of formal legislation is the voluntary agreement, where there is usually a formal legal document recognising that an agreement has been voluntarily reached, but the agreement itself does not actually go through

---

* The terminology 'Green Paper' and 'White Paper' comes from the UK system, which the EU has adopted, but the essential process of a tentative policy paper (green) followed by draft strategy legislation (white) is common across most political systems and processes.

a legislative process. Voluntary agreements go in and out of political fashion. When in favour, they are seen as a quick and efficient way for the participants in the scheme and for the politicians to achieve action without the deadening hand of legislation; but, they can also be seen as an ineffective and toothless mechanism that fails to get results.

Voluntary agreements work best when there are three factors present:

- There is a small number of players that all agree to sign up – an agreement that cannot identify all the players, or only covers 80 per cent of the market, is not good enough.
- There is a solid system for measuring and monitoring progress, ideally done by a third party.
- There are clear sanctions for not following the agreement, for example the threat of imposing legislation and naming and shaming companies in the media that are not performing.

DEALING WITH THE UNFORESEEN

So far, I have tried to simplify the political world and the political process. In the real world of politics, however, it is the people and events that are important, and unexpected things can happen. The formal processes just give lobbying a framework, but you have to be prepared for some surprises.

It is therefore key to start early. It is human nature to

defend what you have prepared, so you really want to speak to officials before pen has been put to paper, as they have nothing to feel protective about. If they say, 'Come back when we have prepared a draft and we can talk then,' you will have a much harder time of it, as the lines have essentially been drawn. Discussions can be frustrating during the pre-draft stage, as officials are loath to publicly agree or disagree with your ideas. You may feel that you have been getting nowhere, but you have to have confidence in your arguments and see what actually comes out in the draft. However, no matter how prepared you may be, politics will find a way to catch you off guard – so always expect the unexpected.

Firstly, the process can be short-circuited. When Emmanuel Macron decided to reform France's labour laws just after he was elected into office in 2017, he ploughed right ahead with legislation without formal consultation, issuing a Presidential Decree in a matter of weeks and side-lining the legislature. This was an exceptional case, but it still did not prevent people lobbying – they just had very little time to do it in.

The process can also be stretched. An emerging law can bounce back and forth through the stages like a game of snakes and ladders. If a minister wants to avoid making decisions, but still wants to be seen to be taking action, the 'we are looking to take strong action and have launched another study and will consult widely with stakeholders' game can be played for years.

Further, leaks can add unexpected stages to the process. Leaks are tactical and rarely happen by accident – although sometimes documents really are mistakenly left behind in taxis. Officials may leak papers just to see what the public reaction will be – an unofficial consultation in all but name. A European government might leak a draft EU document because it is failing to get its way in intergovernmental discussions happening behind closed doors. Or leaks can be aimed at embarrassing decision makers into taking action, or indeed trying to stop them.

Lastly, the process may just die away. In 1999 there was a huge transatlantic row about aircraft noise. The EU, pushed by noisy demonstrations at Frankfurt and Heathrow airports, imposed strict aircraft noise limits. The Americans came up with a technical 'hush kit' fix to make aircraft just quiet enough to meet the new limits, but the Europeans cried foul and banned them. Cue a big row. But, in the end, no one really wanted a transatlantic fight. Instead, everyone went quiet about the EU limits, while the EU came up with a new law in 2002 that fudged the issue and it passed almost unnoticed through the EU political system.

This solution was not immediately apparent when everyone was picking up their cudgels for a fight, but it illustrates how solutions emerge and how politics and political processes can adapt. As the adage goes, politics is the 'art of the possible' and you need to be flexible in order to cope with its twists and turns.

GETTING HELP

DO YOU NEED IT?

The emphasis of this guide is on self-help. You and your team are operating at the forefront of lobbying for your interests, and that should be your focus, as doing it yourself is the most effective way. But getting outside help – for example, on strategic advice, arranging meetings, researching and monitoring events – can augment your resources and spread your reach and influence.

Good help is not cheap, but you can make sure you are spending your money wisely by only paying for what you actually need.

The basic capabilities you need for lobbying are:

- strategic objective setting;
- tactical skills in order to approach and engage with politicians;
- the ability to secure meetings and present your case;
- networking skills for creating and maintaining contacts with decision makers and influencers;
- intelligence and monitoring capabilities; and
- research skills.

You can get help on all these capabilities from:

- an in-house lobbyist or lobbying team;

- a specialist lobbying consultancy;
- a chamber of commerce or business association (e.g. CBI in the UK or MEDEF in France);
- a sectoral business association;
- government department; or
- your local parliamentarian.

You can get help from one, or mix and match them all depending on your situation. The minimum you need is good intelligence on what is going on.

The expensive options are to hire an internal lobbying team or a consultancy (which can do everything in this guide). Even if it is expensive, this may be the sensible option if you are permanently facing high political risks, potential crises and a heavily regulated environment.

Business associations, chambers of commerce and sectoral associations vary greatly in cost. In Washington DC, the costs of associations and industry groups are extravagant and measured in the hundreds of thousands of dollars, while in Europe, costs are usually quite moderate and are in the tens of thousands range.

The good news about dealing with government departments and your local parliamentarian is that they are essentially cost-free, but the obvious downside is that they are dealing with everyone else at the same time. Even so, they can provide excellent advice and guidance, help with securing meetings and, if they are well plugged-in, can give you the heads-up on emerging problems.

CHOOSING YOUR HELP

A good way to look at what help you need is to assess where you are regarding the six lobbying capabilities and target your investment at your weak points.

Consultancies come in many shapes and sizes. The large consultancies can offer the whole gamut of services – they have experienced lobbyists that can provide advice on strategy and tactics and they are backed up by a lot of bright young things who are great at research, intelligence and monitoring. They can also provide geographic reach with offices dotted around the world. Their weaknesses can be that: they lack the depth of knowledge in specific sectors; they lack business experience and dealing with businesspeople; and they are often busy dealing with a lot of clients and can be overstretched.

Boutique and specialist consultants lack the broad offering of the large consultancies, but they make up for this with close client support and in-depth knowledge of a specific sector.

Some consultancies blur the line between themselves and associations by actually running and manning associations on the behalf of companies. This is a good deal, as although the 'secretariat' of consultants is prone to personnel turnover, they bring energy to their work and you can replace them if they do not.

Associations should also be able to provide all the political capabilities. The emphasis is on 'should', as associations and their staff are a mixed bag from the very good to the set-in-their-ways and cynical, who act more like bureaucrats than industry people.

Ideally you want an association to be well-versed in your industry, active, focused and as good as a consultancy, but lighter on the pocket, as you are sharing the cost across several companies.

If you have an association that does not have the lobbying capability, combined with leadership that is unable or unwilling to adapt and change to provide the capability, you have two choices: set up a new association or engage a consultancy to provide the services instead. Experience has shown that a third choice – to restructure and turn an association around – is a huge effort that rarely works and is never quick. Mostly you are just chucking good time and money after bad. It only really works if all the members of an association are equally frustrated and willing to act.

You have to hope you are lucky to have an adaptable and energetic association to work with. Work closely with them and encourage them to get better and better at their job.

GETTING BEST VALUE

A good-value in-house lobbying team, consultancy or

association will be well-informed about your business, your priorities, your strategic goals and what you expect from them. In addition, they must actually communicate effectively with you.

You need to take time to properly brief your consultant or association on your business, priorities and strategic goals. None of this time is wasted, as they cannot really know what your expectations are, what you are looking for or whom you want to meet, unless they are properly briefed. Badly briefed external help can only be inefficient and costly. Indeed, sensible in-house teams, consultancies and associations should be actively looking for opportunities to be properly briefed.

Now, on to the communication. Events are always happening in the political world and you can end up with an endless stream of information and emails as your external help are busily monitoring and reporting back on political happenings. Raw, undigested political news is not much good to you, as its implications are not clear and it is written in difficult political jargon. You need it to be refined, made digestible and, critically, to know what is important to your company in plain language.

A typical example would be receiving a report about a political fight that prevented a committee from reaching a decision. This is always fascinating news for the politicos and policy wonks, so you will receive a detailed report of what happened and the personalities and parties involved in this 'important' political event. But for you, the fight and the personalities involved are only of passing interest. All you need to know is whether the delay in the decision-making process is terminal or temporary, and if it makes a difference to your strategic or tactical goals.

A well-briefed in-house team, association or consultancy attuned to your interests will know only to report what matters to you in jargon-free language. You avoid being inundated with emails and briefings where it's easy to miss the important points among all the political noise.

Ineffective communication is a prime cause for companies not getting full value from the people employed to help them through the political maze. If you cannot understand what they are saying and why they are saying it, how can you value their work?

The political situations faced by individual companies vary enormously, so there is no easy one-size-fits-all approach to structuring your political help. Your company's interests will also vary if it restructures and enters or departs markets.

Regularly reviewing your structure of political help in relation to the capabilities you need and the tools and resources you have will keep your structure up to date and capable of providing high-quality political help.

In summary, when you need help, assess where you need it, choose the right people to help you, brief them thoroughly, insist on good briefings and regularly review your set-up.

Last but not least, when planning and preparing yourself for the political fray, is to have good intelligence.

INTELLIGENCE

DO YOU KNOW WHAT IS GOING ON?

You are literally wandering around in the dark if you do not know what is going on.

The Duke of Wellington, the victor at the Battle of Waterloo, cut to the heart of the importance of intelligence when he said, 'The whole art of war consists in getting at what is on the other side of the hill.'

Good intelligence means you are not only prepared for what is over the hill, but you can also anticipate what could happen next and stay one step ahead of the game.

What you do have to get used to is that there are no certainties in political battles and this can be frustrating for businesspeople who like to have a clear indication of what the next steps and final result will be.

To help with analysing intelligence and when explaining political scenarios, I find it useful to set down the most and the least likely scenarios. This framework makes it easier to picture the possible future and understand why it is not possible to guarantee a given outcome.

Political storms do not come out of clear blue skies. There is always an early warning, you just need to ensure you can hear it. You do not have to set up a secret service or become a news junkie. Firstly, make sure your company not only has its head down focusing on business, but is looking up as well. Are you getting feedback on what people are hearing in external meetings with customers, parliamentarians, journalists, associations and trade conferences? And are you or your team reading the media, trade press, and scientific and conference papers? Have you looked at what your ministry is doing – for example, consultation exercises? When you are reviewing the market, do you include a review of other market influences like regulatory and political risks? If your industry is under political attack or is highly regulated, you would be foolish not to regularly review political risk. All businesses should make sure that there is some process to keep an eye on the political landscape, and if undertaking a major project – a new product or a new overseas factory – should definitely assess the political implications. It is not enough to just assume that no political red flags will be raised, just because they have not been raised before.

If you are embarking on a political campaign or a political storm is coming your way, you need to reinforce your intelligence capability. Are you and your team capable of following political developments in detail? If not, there are alternatives to employing specialist help, like ensuring your trade association is actively gaining and communicating intelligence. If that does not work, there are specialist companies that can provide intelligence and early warning services.

However you do it, spending time and money on good intelligence is a sound investment; ignoring the need for intelligence is an expensive mistake.

While we are on the subject of intelligence, governments

are also gathering information and they have enormous resources to do it. Trade is an important question of state and governments do ask their intelligence services to monitor developments. You can sometimes use these resources – the CIA website is a good source of basic facts and figures on countries.

Once, during a trade spat between Japan and the US in the 1990s, we found out that the US intelligence services had been listening in to telephone calls with our colleagues in Geneva (the seat of the World Trade Organization). We were mostly surprised that the telephone tapping had been so clumsy. Diplomatic complaints were subsequently made to Washington and an article with the story came out in the *International Herald Tribune* containing an apology. What was intriguing, though, was that it was the only press story on the issue. I thought it would make for good 'spies get caught out in trade war' articles, but no subsequent stories appeared. The lesson I learnt was that governments are good at intelligence and, if you do get mixed up in a highly politicised issue, it is better to assume that you are being monitored.

So when you are putting a campaign together, set clear goals, work to your strategic strengths and assess your situation objectively. Choose sensible courses of action aimed at specific decision makers, keeping your planning flexible and momentum going. Get external help when you need it and, above all, stay informed and start early.

POLITICAL PERSPECTIVES

There is a wide choice of options on how you can take political action, but the objective is the same – how to make your views known in your political arena, so you can gather support and convince people to act in your favour.

Another way to put it is that it boils down to perceptions – you are out to change how a political arena perceives you.

At the heart of any campaign is meeting the politicians who are making the decisions. It is so important to get this right that there is a whole chapter devoted to it later on. But what else can or should you do to supplement your face-to-face meetings? Should you have a website? Hold a press conference? Brief journalists off the record? Host a conference? Find speaking opportunities? Prepare a brochure?

The goal is to influence the perception of the players in your political arena – the groups of politicians, organisations, associations, think tanks, academics, pressure groups and businesspeople who have an influence on, or are involved in, the political area you are lobbying in.

If your lobbying is aimed at a small group of officials taking a single decision, you do not need a full-on communications strategy and plan. But if it gets any more complicated, you do need to think about how you are going to use political communications to your advantage.

The whole point of political communications is to make yourself known in the political arena and influence how you are perceived. That arena may already be crowded, or disparate and disjointed so, depending on the situation, you may find yourself elbowing your way through a crowd to get noticed, or, on the contrary, working to create your own crowd.

Depending on your resources, it is usually more practical to work with an industry association or an alliance of like-minded companies when building up a profile in a political arena.

SOCIAL MEDIA

Social media draws a lot of attention. Some see it almost as a magic wand that can achieve political goals all by itself and think that any 'modern' political campaign must include social media. It is not magic, but it is true that an association or pressure group without a web presence will not be taken so seriously.

What social media is, is a great new tool to use for

communicating with a political arena. Politicians and campaign group have taken to it fast, as have trolls and online abuse. It is just not a bed of roses – there are nasty thorns and rotting compost out there as well. You should always have a clear idea of what you are doing and what you want to achieve before assuming that social media is your tool of choice for a political campaign.

Remember that lobbying is hardly universally loved and respected – people are suspicious of it, even in the most lobbying-friendly countries like the US. If you can probably count on getting negative press coverage for lobbying activity, why should it be any different in the social media world? It is also global. A tweet stating 'We lobbied x really hard and successfully changed policy on y' will be seen by anybody monitoring you on the internet and can potentially be used against you. Gone are the days when communications could be kept in one neat national or sectoral box, and you could assume that what you were saying in Washington DC was not being noted in Brussels and Warsaw. This puts pressure on you to make sure that all your public messages are consistent, otherwise you will be variously accused of hypocrisy, perfidy and confused messaging.

With that warning in mind, social media is indeed a great tool to use.

One way to look at social media is to divide what it is really good at into three parts: communication on who you are and what you are doing, via a website, blogs and tweets; dialogue with followers, stakeholders and association members; and calls for action.

Plain communication on a website is relatively passive, as creating dialogue is not the main point of the site. Instead, it is an important tool for companies and especially for associations to tell the world and their members what their mission is, building up their authority on a subject and engendering trust with a broad range of stakeholders.

Tweets and blogs publicising the latest academic papers of interest, an upcoming parliamentary debate or details of when the next conference is happening are excellent ways to show that you are a player in the political arena.

Personally, I do not see much point in someone lobbying going for the rather egotistical 'look at me doing something' tweets – they are still communication in a way, but probably best left to politicians. A good way to tap into this is to hold an event that politicians really want to be seen at and then let them do the tweets and publicise the event for you. Your objective will have been achieved, as the politicians' tweets will show that the event is politically significant. Making it a politically attractive event is the key. Take the defence industry as an example – an event with a room full of missiles and tanks is not going to attract a wide range of politicians, but a room full of young apprentices working in industry will.

Probably the greatest sin is a website where the 'latest news' page or most recent blog post was made many months ago. Why should people come back to the site when nothing happens on it? And more tellingly, why should they think that the people hosting the website are worth following or listening to? Moribund 'graveyard' sites are symptomatic of a campaign plan where the communications aspect is treated as an afterthought. It would almost be better to have nothing, but that is not really an option now that all serious players are expected to have some sort of web presence.

Using social media for dialogue is the next step up from publicising something like a conference, opinion poll, academic study or parliamentary debate, to actively encouraging dialogue by asking people for their reactions: 'Have your say'; replies to tweets; or, 'Let us know how it goes on hashtag x.' This is a powerful way to build up a sense of community among your stakeholders – like-minded people interacting, sharing and conversing on the same issue or subject. The objective is to build and engage with the online community of the organisation and its supporters. Is your association doing this?

Lastly, building on the communication and dialogue, is going out to get your supporters to take action by attending events and actively engaging in advocacy campaigns.

Social media is a tool which can be used to convert informed individuals into members of a community, and then activists.

If this sounds outlandish, have a look at campaign groups' websites – at least the well-designed ones. Everything is there on the opening page of their websites: information on the danger or threat that the group is fighting against; information, like poll results showing that the majority share the same values as those clicking on the site; a lot of inclusive language and calls to join and contribute to the community by making a donation or becoming a supporter; and showing you how you can take individual action immediately, by signing a petition or participating in an email campaign aimed at politicians.

The trick is rapidly building trust and authority, creating a sense of community and safety in numbers and pushing on to show how they, as an individual, can take action – as this was probably a key motivation for them seeking out the website in the first place. For example, put it into words such as: 'We are up against organisations with multimillion dollar budgets, but we've got courage, facts and people like you. Will you become part of our campaign and help protect the planet?' A message that taps into powerful motivators for people – community and the need to be able to make a difference.

This use of social media is tailor-made for campaign groups to attract, motivate and mobilise large numbers of stakeholders for political ends, but it does not mean that it is suitable to be used the same way by associations and companies. Associations have to be selective with whom they are trying to motivate and mobilise to advocate for them, and they need to be careful about whom they inform that they are actively lobbying.

Companies have to be doubly careful, as urging their workforce or stakeholders like customers and suppliers to lobby is tricky to say the very least. There has to be complete confidence that the interests of the company and those of their stakeholders are totally aligned, and that the workers themselves believe that it is right that the company is involved in political lobbying.

Companies and associations are on safer ground when its web presence regarding a political issue is aimed at information sharing and building trust and authority.

Make sure your association is actively using its online presence to reach out to the policy makers and influencers (i.e. corporations, trade associations, pressure groups, think tanks and the media) that make up the political arena, by:

- promoting their vision, mission and reputation;
- establishing themselves as the experts;
- creating networks;
- sharing intelligence;
- building a sense of community;
- showing that they are part of the political conversation; and
- shaping the online policy environment and public debate.

It is always tempting to play it safe and put as much information as possible in the 'members only' part of the website, but you should instead focus on the public side. The point of an association's online presence is to attract, engage and impress a wider audience, not just its members.

In order to do this, you should:

- incorporate social media tools into the overall communications strategy;
- set clear goals for what you want social media action to achieve;
- use it to present solutions and so influence the agenda;
- exploit the potential of infographics and videos for transmitting messages and information;
- make sure what goes up is newsworthy and interesting, repeatable content – not guff;
- always make information cogent and digestible – for example, sum up the subject in ten seconds in a way that will attract politicians, with more detailed information available that will keep the detail-orientated officials happy;
- use key words and succinct statements: create a story, and avoid jargon and overused words;
- be human, as your message and website must resonate – if your website feels and reads like the technical language in a 'how to' instruction manual, you are on the wrong track; and
- invest in it – if using social media and your website is just an afterthought or easily forgotten chore, your stakeholders will quickly ignore or forget you.

CHANGING THE PERSPECTIVE

The old adage 'a picture is worth a thousand words' is something that should never be forgotten when you are looking at how to encapsulate or illustrate a political message.

Working on your website and social media presence should have already challenged you to use imagery to illustrate your mission and messages. It is not always easy, as political problems faced by companies are often detailed and explained in learned papers, dense with industry jargon. How on earth are you going to sum up your issues in an image? In parallel, how are you going to turn your problem into a one-line sound bite anyone will understand?

In a classic political problem, you could be faced by politicians who want to do something that you not only disagree with, but also doubt your customers would be willing to pay for. In this linear 'politician-to-companies-to-consumers' perspective, you are the one seen to be blocking the politicians and the overall progress. However, if you change the perspective to a circular one, with consumers linked back to politicians to make an interrelated cycle, you can emphasise the importance of the consumer to the politicians and make a stronger case.

To put it another way, you are trying to illustrate a political ecosystem that links all the participants – a 'natural' system that more easily lends itself to imagery and explanation, into which it's easier to introduce more participants like suppliers and so further change the perspective of politicians. Not only will companies be annoyed, but consumers (who vote) and suppliers (who employ people) will also be annoyed as well – something that politicians prefer to avoid.

This changing of perspective, or how to better encapsulate and sell an argument, is central to improving your communication in the political arena. You are not in your comfort zone as you are when explaining technicalities within your organisation, to your suppliers or with knowledgeable customers. You now have to communicate with politicians and other players in the political arena who know little to nothing of your business and the technological challenges you face.

How would you explain your problem to a child? This is always a good starting point, as it gets you thinking about the problem from the vantage point of the other side and what could be important and valuable to them. A much better position than 'How do we educate politicians so they really understand our problem?' This is a common and unfortunate mistake, as the tone of communication inevitably comes across as defensive: 'What we are saying is right and you are wrong.'

The 'great communicator', US President Ronald Reagan, put the problem neatly – 'If you are explaining, you're losing.'

Another brilliant orator, US President Bill Clinton, was skilled in that when he spoke to audiences, he did not just talk with the people in the auditorium, but also the world outside. His messages had a wide resonance and that made them all the more powerful and influential.

So when you are looking to communicate, are you speaking to the wider audience, and talking about what's valuable or relevant to them?

To quote the famous cliché about writing: 'Sorry to send you such a long letter, but I did not have time to write a short one.' A short letter takes time to organise, prepare and plan your thoughts in order to get your points across succinctly. In the political arena, you need to take your time so you always communicate well; there is no point doing it otherwise.

THE PRESS RELEASE

The press release is the mainstay of company, governmental and association communications – whether it is sent out by itself or put up on the website, or both. After what seems a lifetime of reading them, I just had to laugh when I saw a cartoon in the *Financial Times* with the caption: 'I read a press release today that was so bad, I ate it!' I'd estimate that 98 per cent of press releases would fit this bill.

So if you have to write or review one, first ask yourself if it would fit seamlessly into the newspaper or broadcast it is being aimed at, and whether the journalist would be able to cut and paste it easily into an article. If it doesn't meet this test, it may be a 'release', but it certainly is not a news release.

The typical errors made in bad press releases are: boring titles; subtitles that go on for a paragraph and are riddled with industry and legislative jargon; even longer opening paragraphs with more jargon and non-news; quotes – if any

– that do not say anything; hedging an interesting newsworthy bit of controversy with so many euphemisms and diplomatic phrases that it is lost on the reader; or one with no real news in it anyway.

The main reason for bad press releases is their approval process – too many cooks do indeed quickly spoil a good broth. Indeed, some of the cooks are actually worried that press coverage might get attention, so they try to delete or rewrite anything that could be seen as remotely controversial.

So keep it short, focus on what is newsworthy and, above all, be prepared for it to make the news. If you'll not welcome the news coverage, or questions from the media, do not write a press release in the first place – it is not the right option for you.

LETTERS TO THE EDITOR

This is one up from the press release and a rather old-fashioned lobbying technique in these days of social media and televised news. But it can be effective if there is a good match between the message and the target audience. Letters to the editor have the advantage in that you are aiming at getting published in a specific newspaper, as it brings focus to the effort. The obvious point is that you have to choose the paper correctly. If you want a political audience to read it, do not aim for the trade press, aim for the papers and media that they will read. In Brussels, probably the most widely read international paper is the *Financial Times*. All

European capitals have a least one 'paper of record' that is essential reading for politicians.

POLITICAL ADVERTISING

Media advertising gets around the big problem of the press release and the letter to the editor – you can guarantee that you will be published, as you're paying for it.

However, you must still make it intriguing enough to get noticed and be read, as well as making a valid point. The worst, in my view, are the paid-for articles that are tedious and boring. I am sure you have noticed and moved quickly on from dense, wordy articles promoting countries and companies in newspapers and magazines. I think the only winners here are the writers and the media owners – at least they get paid.

Advertising – hoardings and posters – take up a lot of resources, but can be effective when aimed at large gatherings. Whatever the advert says or depicts, it is marking out the company as a player to all the attendees.

THE PRESS CONFERENCE

A press conference or an impromptu TV interview can be fraught with traps. A bad press release is quickly discarded and forgotten, but a bad TV interview or press conference can ruin a campaign, or seriously annoy the politicians you are trying to build relationships with.

The classic 'how not to do it' is to fly into town, meet

politicians and then hold a press conference afterwards stating how you think the meeting went, or how you think it should have gone. I could call it the 'controversialist' approach to lobbying – the points may be made and highlighted in the media (which loves a controversy) but how many political bridges have been burnt in the process?

To do the impromptu press comment or political press conference successfully, you have to play it with diplomacy and a keen sense of how you are perceived in the political arena.

The goal has to be firmly fixed on the messages you are trying to impart. Are they coming out clearly, or have you just made sensationalist headlines? If you are attacking the politicians publicly, are you ready for the fight? Governments have a lot of resources and they are the decision makers – are you achieving your goals by potentially estranging them?

You must also consider the perception that the press conference and press interviews will give. Infamously, in November 2008 the bosses of the Big Three US carmakers flew into Washington DC asking for billions of dollars of federal money to help them through economic hard times, but they did so in their private jets. A congressman commented that it was 'like seeing a guy show up at the soup kitchen in a high hat and tuxedo'. Eventually their message did get through, but their press coverage was not pretty and neither was their political reputation.

THE MEDIA INTERVIEW

Dealing with the political press is different from dealing with the trade, business and financial press. They are looking for political messages and you will be lucky to get away with saying, 'I am just a businessperson and only deal with economics.' This can be a good line to get out of commenting on specific party and inter-party politics, but if you are in front of a microphone or in a studio for a political programme, you have to be ready to make your arguments politically, in succinct, plain language.

You have the advantage of being an outsider politically speaking, but you cannot afford to be long-winded or technical. Long statements will be heavily edited before broadcast and your message may be lost.

Jobs and the wider benefit of what you are doing are important; your share price is not. Jargon such as 'seeking efficiency gains' and industry-speak, like referring to problems as 'challenges', will not work. Normal people do not speak like this. Your aim is to come across as a normal person, as the worst outcome would be if you are portrayed and dismissed as elitist, out of touch and only out for your own financial interests.

You have a better chance of coming across naturally if you can do the interview on your own ground rather than in a studio. For example, having a backdrop to the camera shot containing workers and products from your company makes the key point that you are speaking for the business. And acting natural does not mean unpractised. It is very worthwhile spending time getting used to talking to a camera and fielding awkward political questions.

THE 'OFF THE RECORD' BRIEFING

It can be great fun talking with journalists. Like a game of cat and mouse, while you are trying to sell your messages, they are trying their damnedest to find the untold, hidden 'inside story' angle which will give them the scoop.

But like any game, it is vital to agree the rules before you start to play. Will you be quotable as in your 'name, title and company', are you 'an informed source' or a 'person close to events'? It is vital to get agreement beforehand, as sometimes you will give them a tasty piece of gossip or newsworthy inside view that the journalist will suddenly want to validate by quoting you by name or company.

When this happens, you have to stick stubbornly to whatever was agreed to at the start. Remember, the quote may well make an excellent article, sell newspapers and keep the journalist's boss happy, but you will get into a world of trouble if you are named and did not want to be.

Journalists are usually reasonable in such situations, as they do not want their reputation to suffer for not playing by the rules. Who else will want to talk to them if you spread the news that they are untrustworthy? However, if you have not agreed on the rules up front, all bets are off and they have every right to take whatever you said and quote you as saying it.

There is no such thing as 'off the record', so get the rules of engagement straight and mutually agreed before you start playing the game.

If you are quoted in the press and your name, title and company are correctly stated, you will have no leg to stand on when you try to profess to colleagues that the whole thing was 'off the record' and you hate the journalist for being underhand, untrustworthy and scheming. The damage has been done and you might have lost your job.

THE STREET DEMO

Political street demonstrations are commonplace. Students, trade unions, farmers and peace campaigners have all used demos to good effect to publicise their causes. But demos by companies, you ask? I remember a street demo by the US car industry in Washington DC, complete with placards, attracting TV coverage – but the effect was totally undermined by all the demonstrators wearing smart, well-polished loafers. DC lobbyists they probably were; angry, honest citizens they certainly were not. It was the shiny loafers that attracted the cameras and scornful commentary, while the placards and their messages were ignored.

If you are trying to get press coverage and to burnish your political reputation, be true to who you are and drop nutty ideas like holding street marches. It is not true that all publicity, even negative, is good. Ridicule is never a good look.

THE CONFERENCE

'Conference' is a catch-all term covering everything from a roundtable discussion, a panel session, an official stakeholder meeting, a parliamentary hearing, a dinner debate, a think tank breakfast meeting, to a full-blown day-long conference. The ingredients are essentially the same: public speakers and some or total control over the format and who is in the audience.

It is, in essence, an assembly of the players in your political arena, as well as a valuable opportunity to make yourself and your views known, and to shape the agenda and tone of the political debate.

A good conference is not an anarchic free-for-all like a street march. It is a carefully stage-managed event.

The first thing you want to make sure to get right is the tone. If you are in a high-tech industry, make sure the venue and fittings are appropriate. An example of getting this disastrously wrong was when an industry put on an evening cocktail buffet conference to show how advanced they were – but they held it in a small dusty museum with no stage or audio-visual facilities. In the packed room, no one could see, let alone hear the speakers, and when the speakers changed, an enthusiastic and very loud brass band set to, drowning out any attempt at polite conversation. Pretty soon nearly everyone had left, half-deafened and muttering that they never even had the chance to have a drink or a bite to eat, because even the waiters could not make headway through the crowd. A memorable event for all the wrong reasons.

Cultural differences can also ensnare the unwary. For example, at an international conference a solution about lunch was never found between the Dutch and the French delegations. The French wanted a two-hour break to allow for a decent meal and informal networking, while the Dutch only wanted half an hour to refuel before going back to formal deal making. The compromise decision to have an hour-long lunch just annoyed both camps.

An hour-long speech is almost too short for the Germans, whereas that is pretty long, but acceptable for the French. However, an hour is a tediously long time for the British who would be happy with fifteen minutes, while the Americans seem to love an endless series of quick-fire ten-minute speeches without any lunch at all. This all goes to say that if you are going to be successful with a conference format you have to know your audience.

At one international environmental conference in Germany, the evening programme promised three introductory speeches in German, before drinks to celebrate a successful conclusion to a whole day of speeches. Wireless headphone sets were handed out for simultaneous translation in four languages – all very well organised as usual – and the audience waited to hear a few words from the hosts before tucking into drinks. After about twenty minutes, the British, Australians and Canadians retreated to the bar next door. After another twenty minutes, the French and Italians gave up being polite and melted away to the bar.

Two hours later, the German speakers were still going strong and the Germans and Austrian audience were still there! I am not sure how they stood it. When the speakers finally stopped, I asked a German friend if she had found the length of speechmaking a bit over the top. She was puzzled by the question, as she thought that they had been quite good – not so much a cultural difference then, as a cultural divide.

To make it a good conference, you must have three equally important and interrelated aims: profiling what you stand for; creating a positive perception of your organisation; and making sure the audience appreciate the event.

If you focus only on the first two aims, you are likely to end up having a conference where all the speakers agree with each other and an audience that agrees with them. All very safe and satisfactory, but the breadth of the outreach to the political arena has been curtailed and, with it, the effectiveness of the event. You actually need speakers who have a different point of view and to invite a wide audience, not all of whom agree with you. This gives the event balance, interest and shows the confidence of the organisation and its messages.

When the European Parliament began to learn how to wield its power in the 1990s, there was a lot of debate on whether European parliamentarians (MEPs) should be invited to industry–governmental policy conferences. It was not just industry that was hesitant – the governments and the European Commission were also reluctant to give the parliamentarians a platform, as who would know what they would say?

The unhappy compromise at one major industry conference was to grudgingly ask a single MEP to speak, but making sure he was the last speaker on a Friday afternoon when most of the audience would have gone home early for the weekend.

It was considered safer this way by the industry association organising the conference, but the result was a slighted and disgruntled MEP, and an audience who thought, quite rightly in fact, that the association's format choices illustrated its failure to move with the political times and its weakening political influence.

A political arena is not a comfort zone. As soon as it feels too comfortable, organisations are probably forgetting that there is not a lot of point in profiling their organisation only to friends and allies in a political debate. You have to try to reach out across the whole spectrum of the political arena to be influential, and hosting a conference is a good way to do it, as you are orchestrating the controlled environment it is held in.

Once the big issues of audience, format and how you will profile yourself have been sorted out, you need to look at controlling your speakers – which is much like trying to herd cats.

It is so important to ensure that clear messages are delivered and that no one runs over on timing. Your audience may appreciate the speaker, but not if they are being kept from their coffee break and even less so if they are being kept from their dinner. It may seem an obvious point, but audiences value events just as much for the networking opportunities as for the speeches, the debating and the question and answer sessions.

Controlling the cats is not always easy, but clear instructions and a firm hand are a help. Politicians are particularly tricky to stop and difficult to restrict when they are in full flow. A rule of thumb is to give them a firm two minutes to speak if you want a five-minute speech, and give them three minutes if you want seven. And never give them more.

Next is controlling the audience. The first instinct is to only invite friends and parties who agree with you, to present a common front, a clear consensus and exclude the extremists and know-nothings. However, if you are in the audience, it is much more interesting and you are far more likely to be swayed in your views when there is a debate with speakers out to win their arguments. Audience participation also makes for a more interesting event – not least as it saves the audience from feeling that they are being lectured at all day.

You must also control the unexpected. The source of the unexpected is usually the uninvited guest – classic moments have included: a drunken journalist grabbing the microphone to loudly insult everyone; a neatly dressed and heavily pregnant lady striding confidently up to the podium to speak and it taking a few minutes of haranguing for the audience to realise that she was in fact a protestor and not just a protesting parliamentarian; and an activist turning up to a lunch discussion between industry types and a group of parliamentarians in a private Parliament dining room (she had in fact been invited along by one of the parliamentarians who mischievously wanted to jazz up the discussion).

The drunken journalist was quickly neutralised by switching off the mike and luring him out with promises of a better drink outside. The pregnant lady turned out to be civilised enough to be escorted out without drama. However, the activist at the lunch was not for budging, but this turned out to be a blessing as the luncheon debate was a lot more interesting and we were complimented afterwards by the parliamentarians for our broad-minded approach and willingness to involve all sides in the discussion.

THE PARTY CONFERENCE

Political party conferences – run for and by political parties at European and national level – are numerous. They are not always open to industry, but if they are, they can be useful as a networking and profile-building exercise.

If there is a problem, it is that at some conferences the parliamentarians and ministers can be hard to get at, as they are in high demand. In the UK, some parties hold 'industry days' to facilitate business access to politicians and increase the attractiveness for companies to attend – but be warned, tickets are expensive and hotel rooms hard to come by.

THE COMMITTEE HEARING

This is similar to the conference in that the players in the political arena will be there and it is a chance to profile yourself. However, you can do little about the tone, as you are not the host and you have no control over the venue (which is the committee room), and although you may have some influence over the choice of speakers, you have no control over who will turn up.

That said, if the chair can be persuaded to put you up on the podium, it is a gilt-edged opportunity to profile yourself and your messages. As the venue is formal and neutral, being up on the podium shows that you are a serious player in the political arena, giving you profile and credibility. Of course, it can go wrong and often does. The most common mistake made by speakers is spending most of the speech talking about their organisation or company.

The audience is not there to hear the corporate advertising or to learn about the benefits of joining your organisation and what it does. If you have roughly twenty seconds to make a positive impression so people will actually listen to what you have to say, do not spend it talking about yourself.

Talk about the audience and the issue at hand. People always like hearing about themselves.

Your job is to grab or spark their interest, connect with them and make cogent points in the time available. If you have two minutes to speak, make one good point, and if you have five minutes, make two good points. If you are lucky enough to have ten minutes, make three.

Too often, speakers try to squeeze as many messages in as possible, meaning that the speech is hurried, making it hard for the audience to pick out the key themes. If you go over time, things quickly get tricky, with the chair either telling the speaker to finish up, or to stop speaking, and this ends up being the awkward moment that the audience will remember, not the messages.

THE ART OF ASKING A GOOD QUESTION

So, what happens if you are not on the podium? You have to ask a good question to get yourself noticed and noted as a player. But this is not easy – you have none of the advantages of being on the podium: the height, a mike readily at hand, your name on the programme or on a placard in front of you, and no one to introduce you to give you credibility before you speak. You will have thirty seconds or less to introduce yourself, make your point and ask a thought-provoking question.

This may sound ridiculously short, but if you have been at

conference and someone asked a question, did you remember who they were, what organisation they represented and their point? And did you appreciate their question? Or do you only remember them for forgetting to say who they were, rushing or mumbling their point, or forgetting to switch on the mobile mike they were given so you could not hear anything anyway? Most common of all, someone will talk for five minutes and is then asked to sit down before they even get around to asking their question – if indeed they had one in the first place.

Asking an influential question is much the same as making an influential speech, just with very compressed timing.

At a minimum, your aim is to make a positive impression with your presence and body language, by being confident and inclusive. Be calm, unhurried and pause before you speak to get people's eyes focused on you. Breathe in, think about what you are going to say and then say it as you breathe out. Ideally, do not focus solely at the chair, but look around you while you speak and do not be afraid to spread your arms to figuratively involve the whole audience. Always remember that over 90 per cent of your impact will come from your body language and tone of voice.

Asking a question is a 'look at me, I am here and I count' moment. Putting forward a solution is a good idea. It is positive, likely to catalyse debate and therefore be appreciated even if people do not agree with you. You have made your mark in the political arena. Job done.

However, socialising and integrating yourself into a political arena, then getting your point across, winning arguments and shaping the debate and its outcome takes persistence.

How do you know you are making progress? Is all the time and trouble worth it? It is hard sometimes to quantify the benefits of becoming a player in the political arena, but it is easier to see when you are not yet there.

A typical reaction from someone who has been to their first official stakeholder meeting is, 'I had the same right to be there as anyone else in the room, but others were getting all the attention and funding opportunities. I was left out in the cold, while the others already seemed to have an inside track to the important people.' It sounds unfair, but having the same rights is not good enough if you are the stranger in the room. The point of socialising and communicating is not only to make yourself known, but influential. You are building your own inside track.

REPUTATION BUILDERS AND BOLSTERS

You are in a good place if you are seen as the experts on an issue and can show that most people agree with you.

'Expertise' can be bolstered by commissioning an academic or semi-academic study. Of course, you are providing the financial resources for the study and if the study is too one-sided or not made by a reputable organisation, it will be attacked as unbalanced, biased and subjective.

A frequent problem with studies is that they are written

by academics – densely worded treatises, peppered with academic jargon and endless caveats. When getting studies ready for the political arena, you need a good executive summary and at least one really good graphic that sums up the key findings. It is this that will get all the attention – few will be taking the trouble to read the whole report.

The 'popularity' of your cause can be bolstered by polls. Polls are prevalent because they take a helpful snapshot of what people are thinking. Pressure groups and political parties are good at using them for the purpose of proving that they have 'the people' on their side (or even better, showing that their opponents are in the minority) and, by doing so, influencing the shape and tone of the political agenda. They are used less often by companies for lobbying purposes, but nevertheless they are a tool that should be considered.

THE FLY-IN

If you have friends and allies, getting them all together to hold a series of meetings in parallel or en masse with politicians can be an excellent way to build a political presence. Working together, you can cover a lot more ground than one could individually. The strength of a coalition is that it is more attractive for politicians to meet with, as they are talking to a bigger, wider and more influential group.

Messages can be less hard-hitting because the point of the meetings is to be seen, showing off your numbers and getting noticed.

THE MASS MAILING

Sending out a standard text in a letter or email to large groups of politicians will not work. What increases your chances is personalising the letters and the subject lines in the emails.

Why are you likely to read an email? If you think it has been sent specifically to you. You will hesitate if you do not know the sender, and you'll swiftly delete the rest. Politicians and their assistants are no different and they get just as annoyed with spam and junk mail.

There was a classic example of getting a mass mailing wrong in the early days of email, when a lobbyist worked out how to send bulk emails – hundreds of emails, ballooned by frustrated replies 'to all' by the parliamentarians on the send list, crashed the European Parliament email system. An exercise in mass annoyance.

If you are thinking about sending a paper or message to a whole Parliament because it is easy to find their emails, think again. They cannot all be important to your issue. Even if you are thinking about sending it to everyone on a specific committee, take a bit of time to personalise each email and make it succinct. Tedious work maybe, but you have decreased the chances that your message will be immediately deleted.

This is quite a list of various ways to get your point across to the people who matter, and a crucial part of which is plain persistence. Use as many ways as you can to repeatedly get your message out.

All these options are potential ingredients in your overall effort to influence your political arena. Purely considering the different options will foster a more comprehensive approach to your communications strategy.

Make sure to be flexible and take the unforeseen opportunities to communicate and engage when they emerge. Join a government-sponsored trade mission. If a conference or hearing comes up, react quickly and see if you can get on the panel. Submit information and views to official stakeholder consultations.

If you are not getting information because meetings are being held behind closed doors, invite the officials to an impromptu off-the-record meeting. Your job is to make the event an attractive one to go to – whether that is the people who will be there, a simple chance for the officials to talk informally with their negotiating partners or just to have a drink after a long day at the negotiating table.

Finally, always check on the venue beforehand. At one fashionable hotel, the lighting was a groovy green, which may have delighted the interior designers but had the unfortunate effect of turning the pink salmon canapés purple. No one ate them and the white wine looked pretty suspicious.

CHECKLIST FOR YOUR CAMPAIGN

1. A clear goal.
2. Simple and solution-orientated messages.

3. A comprehensive communications plan with integrated messaging for events and social media.
4. An up-to-date website.
5. A social media strategy.
6. An unrelenting focus on reaching out to the key politicians, officials and influencers in your political arena.

GATHERING YOUR ARGUMENTS

When lobbying, your 'product' is your argumentation. Without a good product to sell you are not going to be successful in the political marketplace.

When you have planned out your campaign, you need a document that sets out your position, goal and key arguments. It can take many forms and names – 'policy document', 'agreed statement', 'position paper' or 'hymn sheet' – but whatever it is called, it has to be an agreed, clear and concise statement. It is your product that you will be selling.

HOW MANY POINTS CAN YOU REMEMBER?
People you meet want to get a clear idea quite quickly of what you want, and to do this, they need something digestible and cogent.

How many points can you easily digest and remember? You are doing well if you can remember nine. Seven is still a stretch. Five is doable, but three is relatively easy. Kicking off a meeting by stating that you have three points (or less) is a great scene setter – you have been clear and set a goal that is not going to frighten anybody.

Now look at how many points you are planning to deliver.

If you have over three, have a close look at the points, as you want to make it as easy as possible for your audience to discuss and absorb. How do your points measure up to the desired result? Are they all really that important for your target audience? How many are connected and basically saying the same thing in different ways? Are any points actually just background and technical information on your industry or the subject? Can you replace or illustrate any points with images?

Your task may seem impossible when your document has already been shortened to fifteen important points, for example. But if you cannot remember more than five or seven points, how will your audience?

In the end, you still want to have three memorable points to sell to your audience. If they are three big points to talk through, you need to be able to snappily sum them up when you have finished going through each of them.

Further, remember that the most telling point will be the first one you make. Make it a good one, as it sets the scene for the other points. And make sure you end by restating the first point. People listen closest to your first point and then they usually remember the last thing you said, so you are increasing your chances that people will remember your key point if you top and tail the meeting with it.

THE RULE OF THREE

Paring your arguments down to three not only increases your chances that the audience will remember them, but it immediately gives you a cogent structure that is easy to play with when preparing for a meeting.

Open by saying that you have three points that you want to talk about. The audience will not only appreciate that you are well-organised, but you have laid down a marker that the points will be gone through.

Many meetings have been irremediably marred by opening up with the words: 'We want to go through fifteen points with you.' Right away you have made the meeting sound like a marathon – your audience's minds will be closing and they will already be preparing to be bored, bombarded with information and finally left baffled as to what you really want.

Once, I came across one senior official who mentioned indiscreetly that he had met another company on the same subject the day before. He only said this because he owned up to being completely lost after the meeting, as the other company had insisted on painstakingly going through each point of a dense and ultimately confusing position paper with him. He knew the subject was important and he wanted to support the company, but his thinking had been totally befuddled by the plethora of points presented at the meeting. He then thanked me warmly, because I had set out the same arguments in a simplified and structured form that he could understand and, even better for our advocacy efforts, he undertook to brief his minister on them afterwards.

With three points to make, you have a manageable structure to work with. You may well get too involved on one point, but the audience will often ask, 'What was your third point?' to shift the discussion onwards. If, in a similar situation, you said that you had fifteen points to discuss, I would not bet that the audience would be asking eagerly, 'What are the other thirteen points you wanted to go through?'

Having three points allows for an easier decision on which point you will lead on. Also think about what examples best illustrate your points. Examples or anecdotes are so important: statistics are useful in showing that you master your topic, but reeling off a lot of figures will not make a memorable point. It is the well-illustrated story that counts, as people are hard-wired to remember them, while we are usually not so good at remembering figures.

PICTURES TELL A STORY OF A THOUSAND WORDS

Pictures are great – they create an immediate interest, can be studied and discussed, and they stick in the mind.

People may claim that they can multitask, but I have never

met someone who can read and digest a document and really listen closely at the same time. It is one or the other.

If you are trying to make a point, do not try to do this when you have given your audience a document to read. 'As you will see in the bolded text in section two...' means the audience are trying to find and read the text while your words go over their head. If you have to refer to a bit of text, give the audience time to read it and be patient and silent, and ideally wait until they look up and give their reaction.

However, it is much easier working with an image. If you give the audience a picture and say, 'If you look at the picture you can see how complicated the technology is...' you naturally pause to let the person focus on the right area and look up before you continue. An image is a lot easier to take in and remember than a section of text, and people seem to be much happier to be asked to look at images, rather than asked to read through documents.

An extreme example of using imagery to good effect was a Greenpeace video explaining a complicated point about climate change. They chose to have one of their people explain the case by having a key word printed on each article of his clothing – during the video he addressed each point and then took a piece of clothing off, ending with just a sock covering his modesty. Even though he made more than three points, they were made with humour and the video was difficult to forget. A great example of using imagery, a well-constructed argument and humour to make a telling case.

Stripping off to make your point is not for everyone, but the most successful 'arguments' papers I have put together were made up completely of images on a single page.

GETTING IT WRONG

One always learns more from mistakes and hearing about muck-ups is much more fun, so here are a few learning curves.

A US company launched into a meeting with the UK government by saying, 'You have to buy our product because we won World War Two for you.' Needless to say, this went down like a lead balloon, and what is even more damaging is that this was a memorable (and highly repeatable) phrase that the company was associated with for a long time.

Another regretful opening gambit – 'Why! You are both lovely, beautiful ladies!' – came from an older German man to two young and exceedingly bright ministers' advisors. Astonishingly, he mostly got away with it and the meeting went well, but mostly because we succeeded in keeping him silent for the duration.

In another example, a news radio programme began with an interviewer stating that there were serious concerns being made about the environmental and economic impact of a US company's newest product, a genetically modified organism (GMO). The company representative pooh-poohed the statement by replying that they had done all the necessary research, that the research was confidential and that there were no real concerns in their home market about GMOs in the US. The company representative was promptly slammed in the interview, labelled arrogant and only succeeded in inflaming suspicions about GMOs.

The last example came out in the opening stages of the European political row about GMOs. A disastrous start for the company and the GMO industry that betrayed a badly thought-out campaign based on the flimsy premise that 'trust us' and 'European politicians will have to act the same way as our politicians' arguments would work.

The 'trust us' argument never works, and saying that the workings to back up your argument are confidential is a double no-no. To add that 'our legislators are not taking action' shows an implied disrespect for the political responsibilities, ambitions and attitudes of other political regimes. All in all, it was a grave error of judgement by the company when putting its points together, even if they were short and cogent.

WINNING WAYS

Explaining the challenge of setting and pursuing a political goal with clever tactics can get a bit overly theoretical, so this chapter looks at actual campaign strategies that succeeded. They may not all have been clear wins, but they definitely shaped the political debate and illustrate how groups and organisations allied their commercial goals with political forces.

This is quite a disparate group of case studies and campaign techniques – from technocratic to the highly politicised, and from ones solved within weeks, to those fought over decades. What the campaigns all share in common, though, is the effort to portray their actions as being motivated by higher aspirations rather than just their profits or selfish interests.

WE CREATE JOBS
Job creation is a favourite theme, but a valid and central issue

in the debate in the UK over expanding London's Heathrow Airport.

The debate has certainly not been won, and has being going on for over thirty years. In political terms, the dispute was originally between the local residents objecting to the noise and those wanting to fly – the man in the street everyone could relate to, pitted against the elite jet setters and business interests that people did not really sympathise with. The expansion campaign was going nowhere.

What went a long way to changing this was a switch in tactics by Heathrow – it started to talk about and promote the people working in Heathrow. An airport is similar in some ways to a hotel – everything is done by an invisible army of people who are purposely kept out of the view of the guests. It just happens (in the case of Heathrow, with the help of over 76,000 workers). Further, instead of emphasising business flights, the airport talked about families going on holiday.

The terms of the debate had shifted in Heathrow's favour. The voices of local residents were not the only ones with popular legitimacy – how about the workers, and the families taking well-earned holidays?

WE ARE THE NATIONAL CHAMPIONS

This is another favourite stratagem and one that works well in the nation-driven politics of Europe. European institutions are meant to be striving for the good of Europe, so arguing for national champions is not usually overt, but it is in fact one of the strongest political forces in the European system and a powerful card to play, if you are in the position to play it.

In 2014 this card was subtly played during a debate in the European Parliament over a technical and rather dry climate change law about greenhouse gases used in supermarkets and air conditioning. It also dealt with electricity transmission, but this had been largely ignored in the debate.

The debate was expected to be a typical match-up between environmentalists, with support from northern European governments who were pushing for bans, against industry and southern European governments (who appreciated the need for cooling more than the north). The key swing vote was a bloc of French parliamentarians – which way would they go?

The cooling industry was pretty confident that the French would oppose the bans, as they had met them and thought that they had got their solid support. But, on the day of the vote, the French dropped their opposition to blanket bans, opting for bans that covered only cooling equipment, while excluding electricity transmission. Dismay in the cooling industry! What had happened?

The overlooked electricity transmission business had woken up to the danger of bans that might include their industry, and not just supermarkets and air conditioning. Their industry is made up of national near-monopolies, and they played the national champion card. They said to the southern European parliamentarians, 'Do not outlaw the gases we use in electricity generation as we are the real European industry. Just ban the gases used in cooling as that industry is all non-European – and we need your support.' And they got it. Smart lobbying.

WE ARE THE SMALL GUYS

Sometimes you can turn your small size to your advantage. There is a relatively small industry that rents out equipment like water pumps, electrical generators and coolers – just what you need if, for example, your building is flooded, you need electricity for an outdoor concert or extra cooling for a hospital during a heat wave.

However, legal problems can arise (and this will sound arcane) when you link up a massive cooler delivered by a huge truck to a hospital, as the bureaucrats have a tricky time deciding if this equipment is an 'appliance' or a 'fixed installation'. This matters because there is a whole set of specific rules for 'appliances' – think of things like consumers' rights to take back their TVs and electric toothbrushes to a shop for a refund, or how they are recycled.

The problem the rental industry had was that their equipment had been overlooked in the rule book as their sector was so small. There was a European law that said, if their equipment was classified as appliances, they were now illegal because they contained gases that damage the ozone layer.

However, if their equipment was judged as fixed installations, they would be fine as they came under another law.

So the industry argued that they were the small guys, that their service was vital for public safety and that it was a bit ridiculous to argue that something that had to be shipped around on a big truck could be put into the same legislative box as a household fridge.

It turned out to be a successful argument, even though both the UK rules and the European rules needed to be changed, never mind the fact that the European rules were based on UN rules – so this was quite a thing to re-engineer policy-wise. But it was done in merely three months, with the rationale that it was only a small change to help the small guys and the hospitals. There was no fanfare, little cost and the change saved a business.

WE HAVE TO RUN A BUSINESS

You might find the political message that 'we have to run a business' is a strange one at first glance, but it is the central question and challenge posed when a company closes down a factory or makes people redundant. People losing jobs is never going to be easy to sell to politicians.

Business is, by its very nature, dynamic – there are market peaks and troughs and there is hardly ever a nice, comfortable and steady upward trend in profits and employment. The dynamic of ups and downs is business reality – in fact, the more flexible your business is in dealing with the ups and downs, the better you are able to succeed.

That sounds great within a company and in business schools, but it skirts over the human cost to workers and their families. Meanwhile, in the outside world, the 'bosses' are seen as those who always gain and never lose. Hardly a sympathetic portrait – so how do you go about changing the picture?

The challenge is to be honest, straightforward and human about the business reasons for cutting jobs.

On the business angle, if the cuts are good for the business, where will they also benefit the politicians? This can be hard to find if the reason for the cuts is moving jobs to low-cost countries, but you still need a solid business rationale that makes sense to politicians. They may not like what you have to say, but it is worse if you dissemble, obfuscate or give muddled messages.

On the human front, you have to show that you seriously care for the future of your workers through your actions. If you are closing a factory, have you sought out a buyer for the site to avoid closure? If this is impossible, do you know the local unemployment rate? That is, how likely will your workers be able to find other jobs nearby? A company's focus can be set so firmly on the next business step that the immediate issue of job losses can be overlooked – if they are, the company is forgetting to be human.

You want politicians and the press to be talking about

the business reasons for the job losses. You do not want the debate to be about how heartless and uncaring you are. It will harm your reputation and the morale of your remaining workers.

All in all, cutting jobs is unpleasant and easy to get wrong politically speaking. If you lack, or cannot articulate, a solid business reason for your actions or act callously to your people, you will get slated by politicians and the press.

Finally, if you do cut jobs, make sure that you are not doing it during an election campaign, when any corporate actions will be magnified and your chances of ending up as a political punch bag are much higher – however good your business reasons, or your concerns for your workers are.

WE SAVE THE PLANET (REALLY?)

Maybe I should have entitled this section 'a wolf in sheep's clothing'. Around 2000, a company, whose main business was coal and natural gas, decided there was a potential market for their gas in household appliances such as fridges and air conditioners. The problem was that natural gas is flammable and explosive, and the EU safety standards rules only allowed it to be used in very small quantities, which greatly restricted its use.

The company's solution was to set up an environmental pressure group to argue the case to change the rules on climate change grounds – that it is better for the planet to use natural gas rather than a synthetic (non-explosive) one.

The pressure group certainly made a lot of noise in the normally staid corridors of standards setting, and they looked like they would get their way despite the odds stacked against them. However, the wheels came off their campaign when it became known that they were not a real environmental group.

The point here is that it demonstrates how it is possible to change the terms of a debate. The standards argument was purely focused on safety – indeed, that was their official role – but the lobbying of the fake environmental group to save the planet was successful in changing the ambit of the standards-making body to extend beyond safety concerns to environmental ones as well.

What it also teaches, of course, is that the ruse of sailing under false colours is tempting in the political arena, but any gains will be lost when people find you out – your influence and your reputation will be totally undone.

WE SAVE CHILDREN

When you ride a modern lift, you may not have noticed how they have changed over time, but they have. There are now interior doors and the buttons are low, so that people in wheelchairs and children can reach them. These changes have been made so that everyone can use lifts safely.

From this perspective, it should be a no-brainier that all lifts should be modern and meet the latest standards. But doing this costs money, and governments, which are major building owners themselves, are loath to impose costs on the building sector. It takes a big push to force governments to really act.

Tragically, during a French election campaign, two young girls were killed in an old lift. It immediately became an election issue with loud calls to make lifts safer. The politicians said that they would take action and promptly produced draft legislation to ensure that building owners install modern lifts. This was done in a matter of days, because the lift association had already prepared and handed the government a ready-to-go draft legal text.

The association was the hidden hand in speeding up the whole process – there were no delays in drafting legal texts and thus they got solid political action. The tragedy is that fatal accidents had to happen during an election campaign to prompt action. Lobbying-wise, though, it was the swiftness of the lift association action, because they had already prepared draft legislative text beforehand, that had for once outflanked the powerful building lobby.

WE SAVE THE NATIONAL HERITAGE

The lift modernisation argument brings up the emotive and very difficult question – how much are lives worth? And, as public funds are not limitless, how much money is it reasonable to spend to ensure everyone is as safe as possible?

This is a key debate in preserving lives, but also for infrastructure and buildings. While promoting a new firefighting technology for buildings in France – a high-tech sprinkler system known as 'water mist' – it was thought that objections to costs would be the determining factor in whether the technology would be incorporated into building standards (which are highly prescriptive in France). What was not anticipated was the power and influence of the Parisian firefighters, who were suspicious of a technology that might take work away from their members – the firefighters – who work to save lives, rather than buildings and their contents.

Facing up to or attacking the firefighters' lobby would have obviously been political suicide, so other arguments and decision makers had to be found to get around them.

Water mist is not only excellent at putting out fires, but it also minimises water damage, as it uses very little water compared to fire hoses and traditional sprinklers. This was something that those responsible for museums and historic buildings were very pleased to hear about. A technology to help preserve national cultural treasures resonated in Paris's political circles, and the standards were consequently amended to include water mist technology.

WE FIGHT FOR CONSUMERS

The political fight here was over the right of consumers to buy duty-free drink, cigarettes and perfume when going on holiday abroad. It was also a massive money-spinner for the Irish company that dominated the duty-free shop market at

European airports. The problem for the duty-free business was the creation of the European single market in 1993 – by definition, the single market removed the duty frontier and thus the legal basis to buying duty-free.

The single market may have been created in 1993, but the duty-free lobby kept intra-EU duty-free sales going until 1999. A profitable seven years and all really based on the argument that holiday goers had the right to duty-free shopping when flying within Europe. To put it another way – it took politicians seven years to get over their fear of angry consumers losing their holiday perk.

The industry played on other fears like job losses and the potential demise of small, regional airports that depended on duty-free revenues. Although this did not materialise with airports shutting down or shops disappearing from airports, the duty-free industry did use airports as valuable allies in their fight with the European Commission.

The industry ultimately lost the argument, but the surprise was how long they delayed the axe. And they did it, not by arguing for their commercial interest, but by positioning themselves as the consumer's champion.

WE WANT TO IMPROVE THE LAW

Improving laws is a good and necessary part of lobbying. However intelligent officials may be, they lack 'real world' experience, which can lead to inaccuracies or oversights in law, particularly in the details.

One EU recycling law set out to ensure that electronic appliances used in the home could be taken back to retailers and recycled properly, rather than just dumped in landfill with all the other waste. A relatively simple and laudable aim, but things got messier when you looked into the details and raised lots of questions. Did it mean any electronic appliance, like a computer screen? What happens if the screen is fixed into the back of an airline seat – is it covered? What happens regarding an electronic display for a central heating thermostat – it is obviously in the house, but it is also part of the central heating system, and something you would be hard pressed to take back to the shop when it stops working?

Both of these examples may sound pretty niche, but it meant that the law designed to better recycle consumer electronics like irons and TVs inadvertently got mixed up with aeroplane design and building construction.

The trick was to tighten up the legal language amid a political fight over producer responsibility – that is, how much is a producer responsible for the whole life of their products including their recycling? Simply putting forward arguments that aerospace and building construction should be specifically excluded would have smacked of industry trying to evade their environmental responsibilities.

So arguments had to be couched in terms of making the law 'better' with a boring but much-needed minor technical adjustment that did not mention aeroplanes or buildings at all. In the end, all that was needed was a tighter definition of what was actually meant by the phrase 'electrical appliance' in the detailed depths of the law. Only one key parliamentarian had to be convinced that it made the law 'better' and the adjustment went through unnoticed, but it was in fact an extremely important change.

The lesson is that the dry details in legislation count. Loose legal language can have huge unintended consequences and the only ones out there fighting your corner and correcting textual errors will be you.

WE ARE THE GOOD GUYS

The cosmetics industry are pretty savvy marketeers, but in the 1980s they were out of touch with how consumer attitudes were changing. Campaigns against the use of fur were hitting the headlines and changing attitudes. One company, The Body Shop, was totally in tune with the changing times, with its claim that its products were not tested on animals.

The traditional industry suddenly found angry protestors marching outside their offices. Their response – that they were obliged to scientifically test their products to protect consumers which meant testing on animals – did not cut any ice. Up to that point, 'scientifically tested' was enough to reassure consumers, but The Body Shop's stance changed the public debate. How do you defend testing a cosmetic on monkeys when there are images out there showing the animals in obvious distress? Do cosmetics save lives?

In the public arena, The Body Shop was obviously the

'good guy' and the company was courted by politicians. The traditional industry was furious and hated being the 'bad guy' for following the rules on consumer safety standards.

They won one partial victory, though, as they argued that some of the ingredients in The Body Shop's products had been tested on animals, even if the final product had not been, so The Body Shop had to change its strap-line to 'against animal testing'. Even so, politically speaking, it had run rings round the traditional industry and, in doing so, fundamentally altered the debate about the ethics and politics of cosmetics.

BUT WE REALLY ARE THE GOOD GUYS

You would think that one could not go wrong politically with renewable energy. It is the responsible thing to do in times of combatting climate change. But not everybody likes all types of renewable energy and, in this example, a company found out the hard way that not everyone likes wind turbines, especially in their own backyard.

In many countries, especially those with a low population density like the US, wind turbines or even fracking (a technique to extract gas from rock formations) is acceptable and relatively uncontroversial. An American company operating in the UK, which had a corporate policy to use renewable energy for its factories, did not anticipate problems in investing in wind turbines. Everyone likes renewable energy, right?

Wrong. The factory might have been in an industrial area and next to a busy motorway, and it certainly could not be described as an area of outstanding natural beauty, but even so, this did not stop a parliamentarian in a nearby constituency denouncing the wind turbine project as harming the local scenery. What had been a low-key planning process suddenly became political enough for the company to drop the idea.

It could well have played out differently if the parliamentarian had been briefed beforehand that the wind turbine was symbolic of the company's pro-environment attitude that should be supported by local politicians.

This is admittedly an example of a loss, but it is included to emphasise the point that even when you think you have a winning strategy in place, you cannot assume it will work every time. The company was politically blind-sided, because they had not realised that wind turbines are controversial in the UK, and that political work had to be done to prepare the ground.

WE SUPPORT SPORT

Probably the most famous industry involved in lobbying is the tobacco industry. They have a high-profile consumer product which is addictive, unhealthy and earns them fortunes. Politically speaking, they have declined in influence in Europe with each new wave of anti-smoking laws and restrictions. European politicians are no longer prepared to be seen as advocates of the tobacco industry. But it took a long time – it is a fascinating case of an industry fighting a rear-guard action against the political tides, and a political battle fought in many arenas.

To learn from their example, reflect on how tobacco sponsorship has been associated with the 'health' of sport – would Formula One car racing have survived without its sponsorship? The fact that this is a question of debate illustrates how the industry has successfully shaped the debate away from one based on the question of public health. What has car racing got to do with smoking? Not much, but decades into the political fight, the tobacco industry has successfully used sponsorship of sport to shape and influence the smoking debate.

WE WANT TO STOP CRIME

A company in the UK was in a hurry to sell an old factory, but an essential part of getting the site ready to sell was the completion of an environmental inspection and audit by the Environment Agency.

Sensibly, the company had already engaged with the local office of the Environment Agency, knew the officials and had done the audit process efficiently. Unfortunately, not everyone was happy – the company's bean-counters wanted to complete the process by the end of the quarter, which was a mere ten days away. However, the formal agency timescale stated that it had another seven weeks to process and approve the audit. Tidy corporate accounting was hardly a sufficient reason for the agency to expedite matters. A telephone call was made anyway, but the request was politely refused.

Then the situation changed somewhat – as the factory site was deserted, it had become a tempting target for thieves, who got into the site and stole valuable copper wiring from an on-site electricity sub-station. So, another call was made to the agency – it looked like it was going to be another disappointing rerun, but then the obliging official admitted that he had over fifty case files on this desk and what he needed was a good reason to tell his superiors why a company's file should go to the top of the pile. When told about the theft, he agreed that this was a good reason and official permission was promptly given four days later.

This was not an earth-shaking piece of cunning political gambit, but it was a classic example of corporate 'time is money' culture clashing with the bureaucratic 'follow due process' culture.

The company could not understand why the bureaucrats would not speed up procedures when, in their minds, there was such a good corporate reason – their quarterly figures. It took a knock-back and a burglary to force a change in approach to the agency and to find a way to bridge the corporate–bureaucrat culture gap and leverage a political result.

WE ARE THE SAFETY EXPERTS

In the 1990s, Denmark had been instrumental in pushing the lead-free agenda and had successfully pushed for a European law banning lead in cars with an ambitious cut-off date.

The car industry was crying foul, claiming that all the lead in their cars was already being recycled, so why ban something that was already being reused? This argument did not work as lead was seen politically as an obviously nasty toxic substance. Europe had already banned lead in petrol and, furthermore, the Danish government and environmental groups said that it could be done. But this still left the European officials with several problems – they were not automobile engineers, they did not know where lead was used in cars and they hardly wanted to legislate for unsafe cars, if, as the car industry insisted, lead was a vital part in making cars safe.

They came up with the excellent idea of an escape clause to only allow lead in cars when it was strictly necessary, but in order to draw up a list of allowed uses they still had to ask the carmakers where lead was used. So, in a clever bit of lobbying, the carmakers promptly gave officials a complete list of where lead was used in cars, stating that all the uses were necessary for safety as they were the experts. Their entire list was copied and pasted into the legislation. This was nice work and meant that all the uses of lead in cars had been exempted from the ban.

WE ARE THE PIONEERS

Sometimes companies find themselves in a wonderful position – they have a pioneering and revolutionary product that the politicians like. This was the case in the early 2000s with fuel cells – a wonderful technology used in manned space missions that produces electricity and heat, and which releases water as its exhaust. What is there not to like about that?

Well, some of the traditional power companies were not fond of the thought that their huge central power stations and electricity grids might become stranded industrial dinosaurs. But for the fuel cell companies, they easily found support from politicians and environmental groups and overcame the objections of the powerful incumbent energy industry. It was not all plain sailing, but the key political attraction was that politicians loved the thought of clean 'space age' energy and wanted to be legislative pioneers themselves, and in open forum the traditional industry could not win their arguments to stop fuel cells being incorporated into energy legislation.

WE ARE THE MANY

Numbers are important in politics – as the saying goes, in war, God favours the big battalions. It is a good idea, if you can use it, to portray yourself as representing the many.

Some sectors are made up of many different industries, with many different voices, but this very fragmented and confusing clamour weakens them politically. So how do you turn a weakness into a strength? A good example is buildings – we live and work in them and urban society is defined by them. You would have thought that the building sector would be one of the most powerful forces in politics.

It is politically powerful in some ways, though mainly through inertia. The building sector is huge, varied and disparate, covering everything from owners, architects, surveyors, engineers and estate agents to builders, window makers, bricklayers and plumbers. This is a problem, for example, if you want to improve the reputation of the sector by showing that it is playing its part in saving the planet. This is an important issue when you think of all the resources in energy and water that buildings require – around 40 per cent of all the energy produced is used in buildings.

You can imagine the relief of politicians trying to do something about climate change when a group like the Green Building Council comes along and says, 'Talk to us, we represent the whole building sector. There are many of us, we agree that saving energy is important and we have some great ideas for greener buildings.' The group, by incorporating a purposely wide membership, has turned the fragmentation of the industry into a strength.

WE ARE LOCAL

If you are an international company, how do you get support from local and national politicians?

One US-owned company needed to upgrade a French factory, and its key concern was speed. Renovating and retooling a factory takes time, especially if the factory has things like paint shops and treatment processes, which require official inspections and approvals. French bureaucracy can be a big cause of delays, and delays mean lost operating time and money.

In this case, the company decided from the outset to go out and engage with local politicians from the bottom up. This was a methodical process taking two years or so, with a lot of emphasis on how the company was investing in local jobs, developing local skills and technology with a view to being a successful exporter. This engagement process paid out big dividends when the factory was renovated – all the approvals were properly requested and approved with no delays. While official approval for a paint shop usually takes eighteen months, it was instead done and dusted in three months – the difference to the bottom line of the company was significant.

The company's political groundwork made a real difference. The local politicians did not see the company as a strange, foreign entity endangering jobs, but as a local company they wanted to help.

WE MAKE PEOPLE HAPPIER

Staying with the building sector and the issue of energy, what happens when the actual energy costs for building owners are so low that saving energy produces insignificant financial gains? Why should they do it?

A new argument or motivator has to be found. One campaign focused on a rather obvious observation – people are happier and work better in well-lit, 'green' buildings, rather than in gloomy, ill-ventilated ones. The point was made that working and living in a 'green building' makes people happier and more productive, and the company owners therefore earn more money. Productivity was the killer argument, not the electricity bill.

This is a much more compelling story to take to politicians who are wary and weary of imposing unpopular measures and costs on building owners – not least because home owners vote.

WE ARE THE CONSUMERS' FRIEND

Nearly all markets have quality and safety standards, which have been used by incumbent businesses for a long time to keep unwelcome competition at bay. Standards are their defensive 'regulatory moat'. A new type of standard making was created in the mid-2010s: the eco-design rules. An inelegant name for environmental and energy efficiency standards that hundreds of types of products had to meet to be able to be sold in the EU. Note that these were compulsory – this was not some fluffy voluntary or reward scheme to encourage 'good' products; these eco-design laws went out specifically to ban 'bad' products from the market.

This was an admirable aim, but the idealists did not take into account that eco-design standards could just as easily be turned into protectionist barriers and cause friction between competing technologies.

Some of these standards have reached the political limelight (so to speak) – old-style filament light bulbs are becoming a thing of the past in our homes and halogen lights are rapidly going the same way. All are being replaced by LED technology, irrespective of whether consumers wanted the change.

Looking at how our homes are heated, the traditional technologies burn wood, oil or gas, but the new kids on the block are heat pumps using electricity and renewable energy, making them very energy efficient. It is a fact that even the most energy-efficient condensing boiler burning gas will not surpass the performance of a heat pump that uses electricity and gains renewable energy from the soil or air. Boiler manufacturers got very worried about their technology – would their boilers go the same way as the old light bulbs and be forced off the market?

Cue a big fight which came to a head at a large meeting with all the different industries sat around a table in Brussels. It boiled down to how to label heating technologies so consumers could choose the most energy efficient one.

One side consisted mainly of German boiler manufacturers arguing for two labels – one for the traditional, fossil fuel-burning technologies and another for renewable technologies, as they pointed out that the two sets of technologies were very different. On the other side were consumer groups and heat pump manufacturers arguing for a single label for consumers – the killer point was that the technology did not matter to consumers. What mattered to the home owner was a label showing the most efficient way to heat a house. Putting the consumer first and technology second meant that the single-label argument won the day.

I cannot resist the temptation to mention that the German politician chairing the meeting and championing the two different labels solution was so annoyed by how the debate was turning against him that he tore up all the advocacy papers he did not like – which was most of them – ending the meeting with a pile of torn-up paper in front of him. So if you have a killer argument to hand over, you might want to think about laminating it.

LISTEN TO US, WE ARE RIGHT BESIDE YOU

Politicians have a tendency to pick winners they know or, to put it another way, they can overly rely on what they hear from the incumbent industry firmly seated around the decision-making table.

This was no different when EU officials were deciding to increase the energy efficiency standards for domestic vacuum cleaners. A testing procedure was agreed upon, based on the traditional vacuum cleaner with a dust bag. A new bag-less technology developed by newcomer Dyson, a UK company, was not treated fairly, as its superior technology was marked down by the testing procedure.

This is a classic example of an incumbent industry getting closely involved in decision-making – so close here, in fact, that they were writing the rule book and were able to use the system to disadvantage a new, innovative technology.

Dyson may have subsequently succeeded, against the odds, to overturn the law with a costly and lengthy five-year court case, but the important point is that it had lost the lobbying battle beforehand by failing to be at the decision-making table.

WE ARE TOO BIG TO FAIL

This argument is obviously only of use if you are really big, but the big boys do use it and it works – whether they are the bailed-out banks in the City of London, or large national industrial champions. Big companies employ a lot of people and wield a lot of political influence. The downside is, if you really push this argument you could end up nationalised when you are in difficulties, or have the government as a demanding shareholder whose interests are not necessarily the same as the company's.

WE ARE THE PEOPLE

The internet was hailed originally as a fundamental and positive change to the access and distribution of information – a leap forward for democracy and the power of the individual. The argument that it is all about individual freedom remains the strongest argument for companies hoping to ward off political complications while creating the gig economy and exploiting the potential of the Internet of Things. Politicians will get involved, though – the disruption is too radical to the economy and people's lives for it to be any other way. Even their 'tools' of government, like business taxation systems, are out of date for the new internet-based economy.

The taxi business is a case in point. Faced by new competition from Uber, the app-based business, taxi drivers cried foul and called for governments to variously ban Uber, impose regulations on them or, in the case of London, threaten to take away their licence with the support of the socialist mayor. The political fight will continue, but the strongest argument for Uber has been the sheer numbers of their drivers, who are ordinary working people – why shouldn't they be able to find work if they want to?

All these examples demonstrate how companies need to adopt political messaging to win political arguments. The tactics you use externally for investors and customers – your financial results and advertising (i.e. 'We make money and great products') – is not relevant or telling enough in the political arena. You need to use messages and themes that appeal to and can motivate politicians.

AN AMERICAN IN BRUSSELS

Gershwin's famous piece 'An American in Paris' en-capsulates the feeling that Americans are both exotic and familiar to European politicians – not quite complete strangers, but neither familiar friends.

Americans and Europeans may both have democratic systems with elected politicians, based on similar political philosophies and political institutions, but that only makes them disconcertingly similar.

What I mean by this is that if you rush into Europe aiming to fix a political problem, the political systems look similar to the US at first sight.

The branches of government – the executive, legislature and judiciary – may look familiar, but if you assess and act towards them as you would in the US, you will find the experience confusing. It is best to keep an open mind, stay patient, be prepared for the unexpected, and leave your US toolbox of political tactics and stratagems at home.

US President Ronald Reagan once said that 'The nine most terrifying words in the English language are "I'm from the government and I'm here to help."' If this is the case in the United States, it is doubly so in Europe.

Europe is not the land of small government. Some statistics suggest that in France, one in five workers are in the civil service – about 5.5 million people. Statistics are slippery, but figures from the International Labour Organization has 37 per cent of the workforce of Norway in the public sector, compared to 21 per cent in the UK and 17 per cent in the US.

However you measure it, Europeans rely on high levels of public services and hence high numbers of civil servants to administer them. In matters to do with commerce, governments in Europe are a lot more interventionist. This attitude may be welcome in nascent markets where government support is appreciated, but it is not always the case. You will be surprised by the amount of government influence in markets and by the attitude of European politicians and officials. Few have a pro-business or pro-market attitude or any experience in business. Many are frankly suspicious of markets and market forces, and are more inclined to taking a *dirigiste* or interventionist attitude to business than a laissez-faire one.

Making pleas based on how much something will cost or appealing for the recognition of market realities will not suffice; neither will your share price and earnings. You should be careful in claiming that the US market is open (with the subtext that the European market should be as well). Is it really open? Laws like 'buy American' in federal contracts are well known, so be sure of your ground before you claim the moral high ground when talking trade.

THE US AND EU IN THE WORLD

The transatlantic marketplace is the largest in the world involving 15 million workers and $5.5 trillion in total commercial sales per year. As an American you might be surprised to learn that European companies directly employ 4.3 million people in the US, while American companies employ 4.7 million people in Europe according to a report by the Center for Transatlantic Relations. They trade together more than with any other trading blocs and the two sides are also their largest mutual inward investors. But this does not prevent frequent transatlantic squabbles.

The US and the EU are both friends and rivals when it comes to trading, as well as in rules and regulations, as they are the de facto rule-makers of the global economy. Everything from accounting rules and aerospace standards, to car testing standards, merger approvals and data privacy, one or the other will be the global rule-setter. And internationally, if they are not setting the rules themselves, they are the prime movers in the rules emanating from UN bodies.

The two sides also inspire each other to legislate. Obliging cars to be fitted with catalytic converters to clean exhaust fumes originated in Sweden. It was then copied by California, taken up by the EU and since then has flowed to many other countries around the world. Obliging lead-free electronics followed a similar route with laws originating in Denmark, taken up by the EU and then on to California, China and elsewhere.

It is a fact of life that if you are trading or operating internationally, you are likely to come up against EU rules. It is little surprise then that the biggest corporate spenders in Brussels on lobbyists are the Americans.

THE EUROPEAN UNION VS THE UNITED STATES OF AMERICA

If you look at the public relations material generated by the EU, one might be forgiven for thinking that it is very similar to the US – with an open market for goods and services and people moving easily and readily from state to state to live and work. This is far from the case. The market for most goods is relatively free, but much more restricted in services, and in comparison to the US, there is a lot less movement of people between states. Although there is the European currency, the euro, unlike the dollar, it is not used in every EU country.

You might also be forgiven for thinking that the EU is essentially pro-free trade, but protectionist forces in Europe and indeed on both sides of the Atlantic are strong. If they were not, there would probably already be a transatlantic free trade area. Taking one example, you would have thought that it would not be such a problem to have common rules for cars and trucks, but there is no uniform transatlantic approach. When they tried something simple like lawn mowers, it took twelve years just to agree on a common testing methodology. This is still the only successful agreement on common transatlantic rules for vehicles.

The difficulty is not just down to practical problems like differences between imperial and metric measurements – it also suits a lot of industry, trade unions and politicians to keep the laws different in order to protect their markets. Agriculture, for example, represents only about 2 per cent of transatlantic trade, but it is the purported worries over food – such as chlorine-washed chickens and hormones in beef – that have halted transatlantic free trade talks, and many non-agricultural businesses are quite happy with this result.

Brussels EU is not like Washington DC

The major difference is the money and strength of the US institutions in Washington, whether you are talking about the power of the Supreme Court, the spending power of Congress, the importance of the FBI and other US Agencies, the US armed forces, or the power of the President in foreign and domestic affairs.

Washington DC is a strong centre and in all the aspects I have just highlighted, whereas Brussels is weak, the real power remains in the countries ('member states' in EU parlance). So, depending on your issue, you may have to aim at Brussels, or the individual nations, or a combination of both. With trade and large mergers, aim for Brussels. For tax, energy policy and defence spending, aim for the capitals.

Washington, with its constitutionally ordained system of checks and balances, is practically designed not to reach decisions. Working with it, everyone is used to the back and forth dynamics of Washington. The Brussels rulebook, on the other hand, is designed to reach decisions. Once a piece of legislation is launched, there is an inevitable, almost grinding advance through the institutions. The back and forth is time-limited and progress is hard to stop.

EU capitals are not like Washington DC
The Washington system could be summed up as the President holding the most influential position as the Executive and head of state, but checked and supplemented by Congress and then double-checked by the Supreme Court.

In Europe, there is little of this constitutional neatness and system of checks and balances. Firstly, apart from France, where the President is a hugely influential central figure, heads of state are largely ceremonial and apolitical, whether they are Presidents of republics or kings and queens.

Political power usually rests with Prime Ministers who are part of, or close to, the legislature. And the legislatures themselves vary in importance. In the US, Congress has a major say in defence spending and approving secretaries ('ministers' in Europe), senior officials and treaties. This is not the case in Europe, with nearly all governments having exclusive power over defence spending and treaty-making, supported by a mostly permanent civil service and with a much less politically prominent legal system.

Not all European countries are in the EU

The EU does not cover the whole map of Europe, and you need to check depending on where you are going. You do not want to end up like one American lobbyist, who was really annoyed during a planning meeting to lobby the European Parliament, because there were no Swiss MEPs on the target list. Mistakes can also happen when putting together maps of Europe for lobbying brochures when countries are missed out – for some reason, this often seems to happen to Norway.

National membership of supranational bodies can be confusing in Europe. They are all members of the UN, many are members of NATO, a lot are members of the EU, but a few, like Switzerland and Norway, are members of non-EU trade organisations like the European Free Trade Area. It is important to have a quick check before leaping in.

Europeans are not Europeans

Few Europeans identify as Europeans. Most take their identity from their nation and, many, simply their region. This matters, as getting it wrong in a meeting can sour the atmosphere. If you are not sure, do not try to guess, 'You sound like you are German.' It is inevitable that the politician will be Austrian, or, worse for you, Polish. Same goes for the British – they'll be proudly Welsh, or Scottish; and the Spanish – they'll be Catalans. Guessing is not a good idea, and neither is saying, 'You're European,' or worse, 'You live in Brussels, so what's it like living in Germany then?'

Europeans are very proud of their country, history and culture. If you think that Atlanta is architecturally more beautiful than Paris, keep it to yourself. One American in a hearing I was at did not, and had no idea of the deep offence he'd caused to his hosts.

National and regional identities are important to Europeans, and 'Europe' is too new and too nebulous for Europeans to be identified by it. I am sure that it must be similar sometimes in the States – I was amused by a Tom Cruise film in which the hero asks an army sergeant if he's American, but the sergeant replies, 'No, Sir. I'm from Kentucky!'

Bridging cultural differences and language barriers
It is best to accept that there are cultural differences and that they are not always easy to anticipate. Even if you think that the British are nearly the same as Americans, it is not true. The Irish writer George Bernard Shaw knew what he was talking about when he said, 'The USA and Great Britain are two countries separated by a common language.' They may look and sound similar, but there is a definite cultural

distinction, and this holds true for political culture as well. But this does not mean that differences cannot be bridged – they certainly can be. If you are curious about the country you are in and are patient, you will not go far wrong.

To give a really basic example – when meeting Europeans in summer, expect the meeting room to be hot. Air conditioning is less prevalent than in the US, especially in historic buildings, and even when it is installed it is not set to the cold temperatures you have in the US. So dress accordingly and do not complain about the thermostat setting. A few minutes in to one meeting, an American decided to get up and adjust the thermostat to the 'right' setting – thinking it would be appreciated by everyone. It was not, and the action only served to highlight cultural differences rather than bridge them.

The officials and politicians you are likely to meet will speak English, often to a high standard. But you do have to allow that even if they are good English speakers, they will not necessarily be familiar with American idioms and it is unlikely they will know industry technical terms and jargon. To get round this you have to be disciplined in making clear, jargon-free points, and pause between points. This is a good idea anyway, but it is particularly important in getting over language barriers, as it gives your audience the chance to ask for clarity.

When you make a presentation in Europe, make sure to use metric measurements. It is not that Europeans have something against American weights and measures, it is just

that pounds, Fahrenheit and inches generally have no resonance with Europeans.

Lawyers and the courts
You'll probably be glad to hear that aggressive litigation, class
actions and huge punitive fines are not common in Europe.
There are far fewer lawyers and, on the whole, using court
action as a lobbying tool is avoided. The legal processes are
lengthy in Europe and companies and interest groups have
fewer rights to take authorities to court.

As the French say, 'It is better to have a bad deal than a
good court case.'

Using court action to sue the government for enacting a
law is not an option in Europe, where suing a government is
rarely allowed. To threaten to sue the European Parliament if
it enacts a law is not an option either. This can be frustrating
for US businesspeople who are used to using the courts and
the threat of court action as a forceful lobbying tool.

Of course, you can take the European Commission to
court, but it is not quick, nor cheap. You need to allow about
four to five years for a result. The legal wheels move slowly in
Europe and to take a case to the European Court of Justice
you have to go through a national court first. It is very rare
for a primary piece of EU law to be annulled.

Compliance practices
The ability of US companies to cut a deal with legal authorities

is not the same in the EU. In the US, it may be accepted practice that if you find out your company has inadvertently done something illegal, the company can go to the authorities and make a voluntary 'disclosure' that something has gone wrong and then work out a deal on how to resolve the matter. This option often does not exist in Europe – if something is formally disclosed to authorities, they may not be able to offer a deal and are formally obliged to prosecute.

Make sure of your ground before engaging politicians on a legal or semi-legal matter.

European funds are European, for Europeans

A great source of frustration for US companies is reading about the x millions of euros being given out to companies for research and development in Europe and then being flummoxed by the inability to get their hands on some of the money.

Research funding is not the same as in the US – the bureaucratic hurdles are high and confusing, and the strings attached to the money numerous, and it all takes a lot of time – plan for three years to get things up and running. As money and authorities are involved, the process is political and a good game plan is needed in order to land any funding.

If you are looking at the enticing billion-euro headlines, keep several things in mind. Firstly the money is meant for European companies, not just any companies who would like money for research and development (R&D), and you will need to match the funds you receive. You will be obliged to work with other European companies in a consortium and share the intellectual property generated during the R&D. Further, the rules on guaranteeing that data stays within the EU (including the servers used to transfer data) are getting tighter, and if you are based in the US, it is becoming tricky to even dial into European funding conference calls. And, lastly, there is of course competition for the funding from your European competitors and they have all the advantages of playing at home.

If you have R&D operations based in Europe, you are eligible to try to get funding, but you have to play the European game – use European frontmen and accept that the Europeans will write contracts their own way (whatever your lawyers might say). You should also consider that 70 per cent of public funding in Europe is granted by national governments and you could well find it easier and quicker to secure funds there – but they will still be 'matching' funds obligations and consortia are favoured.

The picture is pretty bleak if you are considering a simple jump over the pond to get your hands on some funding from the European money pot. However, if you are looking to build up R&D in Europe and want to get involved and work with European companies, the system can work in your favour, even if it is clunky and frequently frustrating.

If you are looking for public funding (known as 'state aid') for new investments, factory redevelopment or training, for example, remember that the money will come with strings attached, and that EU countries are restricted as to how much money they can give you through grants and tax breaks to ensure fair competition. You do get more help in this area of funding, though, as countries are keen to see investment dollars entering their economies.

European standards

Standards for products and services are there for many reasons – to protect consumers and the environment are two important ones. However, it is inevitable that what is considered the gold or the basic standard will be based on the incumbent industry's technology and practices.

They may indeed have been purposely constructed to be protectionist, or they have just have ended up that way, as, by the very nature of the process of standards making, innovative or 'foreign' products and services are not taken into account. Nevertheless, European standards committees are in fact relatively open, but a political and diplomatic approach is needed to get either you, or your representatives in Europe, through the doors.

If you are exporting to Europe or starting up a presence in Europe, standards are often the first hurdle you encounter. The processes of standards and 'notified bodies and standards' test houses (the formally authorised standards organisations) can take some getting used to. Just because your service or product meets US standards does not mean that they will automatically be approved in Europe. But, at the end of it, the final approval of the CE mark on your product gives it access to all EU markets.

New trade barriers

It may sound odd, but the European love of banning things is encouraging protectionists to put up more barriers to trade. Bans on GMOs in food grabbed the headlines, but at least there are ways to check if GMOs are in agricultural imports. But, what happens when the banned substance is not actually in the imported food you eat, or in the imported aeroplane you are flying in? For example, if you ban a pesticide that is used while plants are growing, but it is washed off before they are packaged up, or there are banned chemicals used in aeroplane manufacture that are also cleaned off before final assembly.

Consequently, producers in Europe have had to go to some lengths to find alternatives when manufacturing their products, but their competitors outside the EU have not had to – and they are annoyed. Annoyance leads to farmers and industry demanding protection from imports 'made the wrong way'. They are getting a ready audience in the European Parliament, and if the WTO is not functioning well, more of these types of trade barriers will pop up. As an American company, spotting these barriers in time needs good intelligence on what is happening in Europe and the ability to find pro-free trade friends and allies to try to combat them.

Lobbying vs lobbyists

Lobbyists might not be very popular, but the right to lobby is a given in the US. Indeed, lobbying is catered for in anti-cartel laws, which expressly allow companies to work together if they are lobbying – there are no such specific allowances in European law.

The US lobbying 'industry' is well-established and not too many eyebrows are raised if government officials go through the revolving door to work for the other side. Of course, a lot of the people lobbying in Europe are ex-government as well, but it is not on the same scale as the US. Lobbying itself raises eyebrows in Europe.

Some governments do not like to be seen to accept meetings with lobbyists, or corporate representatives, particularly foreign ones. Many officials do not see the point of meeting with industry anyway, and if they do feel the need, they will meet the relevant national association, not individual companies.

Nearly all the US politicians and officials I have met have been positive about holding a conversation with industry people, and often say that it is important for them to hear from industry – even if they do not always agree. It is the opposite in Europe where you do not have an automatic right to be in the room. Often the opening remarks by the politicians in European meetings are a variation on 'This meeting is exceptional, as we never usually meet with industry.'

The difference in attitude can be quite stark when

attending lengthy international meetings, like UN climate change negotiations. The US government delegation is very likely to have semi-formal daily meetings with US business representatives to keep them up to date with negotiations, whereas European companies may be lucky to get a briefing several days after the meeting has finished, if at all.

This attitude to businesspeople, lobbying and foreigners has to be taken into account when you go about trying to meet officials and politicians. Not all of them will accept meetings and your emails and correspondence can be safely ignored. The key to getting through a difficult door is to be introduced by a friend.

Grass roots campaigns

Grass roots campaigning – urging your workforce to send emails and letters to their members of Congress – is a fine lobbying tool in the US, but it really does not work in Europe.

Culturally speaking, Europeans may be political in the sense of their party membership and trade union movements, but this does not include their company or work life. This is sharply differentiated from private and family life, and politics is a private matter. Urging them to write emails to politicians on the company's behalf rarely works and is most likely to stir up ill-feeling.

Finding friends and allies

You can usually find out quite a lot about laws going through the EU system from websites – the EU's system is frightfully clunky, so have a look on the UK government's website, which is usually easier to use. Research gets more tricky at national level, where lack of transparency (how much a government deems it necessary to tell people publicly) and language barriers can make life difficult.

Depending on your success in finding out what is happening, your first port of call should be the relevant country's US embassy, or, if you are going to Brussels, the US Mission to the EU. They can help you find out what is going on and, if you press, the identities of the ministries and officials involved. If you make a good case, they may even help you by meeting the relevant officials to press your case. Other valuable advice they can give is their local knowledge on politics and the industry groups or associations that may be involved, or could be influential on your issue.

In Brussels, you should contact the American Chamber of Commerce to the European Union (AmCham EU) – by definition an organisation out to fight for US-owned companies and also a long-term champion of the European single market. Not all European industry welcomed the single market when it was launched in 1993 and this struggle between free-marketeers and protectionists continues to hold sway in EU politics.

AmCham EU specialises in lobbying the EU institutions and regularly receives awards for being one of the most effective lobbying associations in town. The US Chamber of Commerce, which is a separate organisation, also has a branch in Brussels, giving you another route to get information and advice.

If your organisation or company has offices or factories in Europe, they may be members of the national US Chamber of Commerce or the national sectoral trade association.

The US chambers in Europe are primarily networking organisations, but events like Brexit have pushed some of them into taking politics and political access for their members more seriously – the US chamber in the UK, known as BritishAmerican Business, is a case in point.

National sectoral trade associations vary a lot in how they treat foreign-owned companies. Most UK and Irish associations are pleased to have US-owned companies as members, but in other countries they are not. German and French associations are not renowned for their welcoming attitude and neither are EU-level associations, but you may be lucky.

If this all sounds rather protectionist, it is. You therefore have to maximise any leverage you have, by actively looking for friends and allies.

Attitudes to corporate America

Corporate America is big and powerful, and thus threatening. European politicians assume that corporations, with their money and lobbying influence, control Washington DC.

When George W. Bush refused to sign the Kyoto Protocol on climate change, meetings for US companies on environmental issues in Europe became sticky. Because it was assumed that corporations ran US politics, European officials kicked off meetings aggressively, asking why US companies did not believe in climate change. Not a great way to start a meeting. This illustrates that if the US government is doing something politically unpopular in Europe, companies will be associated with and blamed for it. The best retort is to say that you represent your company, not the US administration.

Where American companies fare better reputation-wise is compliance. If you asked a European politician to rate US companies for their diligence in compliance and processes, they would rank quite highly in comparison to a list of European companies – probably among the Nordic countries. The dangers of being sued in the US are well-known, so if you say that you are arguing for better compliance with rules within Europe, you are quite likely to be trusted.

Attitudes to Americans

'Everyone loves Americans! Right?' Well, not quite.

American culture in the form of TV shows and movies is everywhere in Europe, its corporate brands are well-known and its science, technology and business prowess is well-respected. But this sheer strength, or apparent 'cultural imperialism', can lead European officials and politicians to be defensive, competitive and sometimes aggressive when meeting you and reacting to your arguments.

This is not helped by some Americans' plain speaking. In countries most culturally similar to the US, like the Netherlands, Britain, Ireland and Denmark, plain speaking may be appreciated, rather than taken as being rude, but even there tact and discretion will get better results.

At a diplomatic event, while I was chatting to a Luxembourg politician, an American lobbyist rocked up, interrupted us and immediately went about setting the politician straight on a controversial point of climate change policy. He spoke without pausing for five minutes and, without waiting for a response, turned away smiling to find his next target. The politician turned to me, rolled his eyes and we carried on our conversation as if we had never been interrupted.

Later, to my disbelief, the American told me how he thought that the conversation with the politician had gone really well. It would be an understatement to say that the American lacked a certain cultural sensitivity, but if he had just paused a few times and bothered to engage with the politician, he could have got a good result and not lived up to the stereotype of the brash American.

OTHER ENEMIES AT THE GATES

Calling companies from the other major trading part-ners with the EU 'enemies at the gates' may sound a bit strong, but if you are Japanese, Chinese, Indian or Canadi-an, you will realistically face more hurdles than Americans when lobbying in Europe.

The high level of Europe's rhetoric in support of global trade and welcoming international investment jars with the repeated admonishments by European politicians to their industries to improve their performance for fear of being overtaken and submerged by the incoming tide of interna-tional competitors.

Politicians will do their best to ensure that it is not a level and open playing field for international competition. Import quotas, tariff barriers and non-tariff barriers exist at the border. Even once you are inside, there are local content requirements (for example, if you set up a factory in certain industries, you are obliged to source a specific percentage of parts and components locally), special approval procedures for acquisitions and mergers by foreign companies, restrictions on bidding for public contracts and vetting procedures for infrastructure contracts on national security grounds.

Such defences do add up to the fact that Europe seems to be trying to keep the enemies from the gates, even if you are Canadian, Korean or Japanese with EU free trade agreements in place.

When you engage with European politicians, your problem can be summed up by the fact that people and politicians do not trust people they do not know. If they do not know you, how do they know what your motives are? They will suspect that you are trying to put all your European competition out of business.

The cultural barriers are larger and more difficult to bridge than those faced by Americans. Canadians have the advantage that they are seen as similar to Americans, but the level of knowledge and familiarity with Japanese, Korean, Indian and Chinese cultures is much lower and the perceived threat of their business is much higher.

It is not all bad news. On the plus side, European countries are looking for international investment and there is the lure for investment in the European single market, which has a large and prosperous population.

Even so, to judge that engagement in Europe can be done solely on economic and commercial terms is to ignore the fact that your situation is very political. If you have to reach out to European politicians, you have to be prepared to make extra efforts in explaining your motives in order to bridge the cultural and knowledge gap.

Similar to Americans, what your government is doing has an impact on how your company is perceived. But as they say, money talks, and if you are investing and creating jobs this is solid evidence that you are becoming part of the industrial and commercial fabric of Europe.

Jobs and investment are your strongest arguments to persuade European politicians that you have earned your place at the political table. Persistence and patience are required to allay fears and suspicions in order to become an accepted participant at the political table.

Working with Europeans to help you through the political doors is also a good idea. Just make sure that they have thick skins – once when walking into a room to discuss international Japan–EU cooperation with a minister, I was pulled aside by the minister and asked, 'Why are you working with the enemy?' A strange way to kick off a meeting on international collaboration, but a useful reminder of the real political feelings under all the friendly rhetoric.

Other differences in political culture when lobbying in Europe are the players in the political arena. Parliaments and parliamentarians are important players, not just the national government officials and ministers. Pressure groups and campaigners enjoy recognition and influence, and the media is generally more rumbustious. You must take all of these factors into account when you approach a political problem in the European arena.

LEVERAGING YOUR INFLUENCE

There are two tools you can use to leverage your influence before and during a political campaign: have a good reputation and work with friends and allies.

A GOOD REPUTATION

If you are going to influence anyone, you need to create an attractive persona or profile for your business. It is a fact that people are more easily persuaded by attractive people; it is the same with organisations.

It is definitely harder to persuade people if your organisation is unknown, more difficult if people are suspicious of your motives and harder still if you are hated.

Put this way, the value of your reputation can be taken for granted or underestimated until it is damaged or destroyed.

A reputation can take years to build up and cultivate, but moments to drain away.

A reputation has personality – with values, emotional appeal and relevance. You may think that this list is more relevant for describing a person rather than your business, but this is the point. Machine-like corporations are not appealing as they lack human values, lack emotions and are distant or irrelevant to everyday human life.

What do you think of when you see an image of a green unpopulated expanse of moorland? This is an image often used by businesses as a 'green' backdrop to their marketing material. Personally I love moorland, but it probably has zero relevance to an organisation's product or arguments (unless you are a peat extractor – then the image will definitely be dismissed as 'greenwashing' – the act of making spurious environmental claims). But what using this image illustrates is a failure to understand that you need to create a personality with emotional appeal.

A brand has to appeal to people's values and emotions, and be relevant.

When you are thinking about your product and the political challenges you are dealing with, it can be too easy to get lost in your own details. You have to always ask yourself, what does your product actually mean to people?

You might be arguing with politicians about setting standards for the energy efficiency of light bulbs in offices, the labelling of medicines or noise levels for aeroplanes. This already sounds dry, boring and only relevant to experts.

But it has personality when you start describing that you're fighting for highly desirable places to work in, better healthcare and affordable overseas holidays. You will be seen to be out there lobbying for and delivering things that people want – that's a reputation to have and nurture.

BRING FRIENDS TO THE FIGHT

Also important in leveraging your influence is to gain influential friends and allies.

To play well in the political arena, you have to have an idea of who is in it. Arenas come in all shapes and sizes, but on the whole you will find a similar mixture of organisations. They are your potential friends, allies and opponents.

A lot of the emphasis so far has been on what to do as an individual to tackle political problems. However, the big multiplier in your effectiveness is when you have friends and allies joining you, projecting a broader front which can hit harder than you can on your own.

If you have support at your side during meetings, you are already showing that many players are equally concerned by the policy you are debating, and politicians and officials will take it more seriously. Even if they are not physically beside you, you can refer to them to achieve the same effect. If you are reaching out to many officials and ministers involving many different nationalities, it is best to form an alliance, which you can play to its different strengths.

PLAY BY THE RULES

It is important to note that, when teaming up with friends, outsiders will be suspicious if you are meeting behind closed doors and teaming up in the corridors of power. You need to be whiter than white and above suspicion.

Under US law there is a clear rule that companies can get together to discuss lobbying government. There is no such clear-cut law in the Europe. While associations are definitely allowed to lobby, what you cannot do during association meetings is talk about anything regarding pricing or competition.

Making a broad statement that a law will be costly is fine, but as soon as you make an additional comment that you are confident that the industry could pass the cost of the law on to customers, you are in trouble. This would mean that now the group is talking about future pricing intentions in the market and so breaking competition rules.

This opens your company and the association to a potential anti-competition investigation. Penalties for cartel behaviour are harsh – fines of up 10 per cent of your annual turnover can be imposed, and the damage to your reputation will probably hurt your company more than the fines.

So, when you do team up with friends, stay safe. Formal agendas and minutes have to be kept, as they will be your proof of proper behaviour if the inspectors come calling. Make sure you do not become partners in crime, or are even suspected of being so. Check that, when you are discussing lobbying, everyone around the table knows about the dangers of anti-competitive behaviour and what they can and cannot say. Suspicions are enough for your enemies to smear all of you.

If you get it wrong, you risk the authorities turning up unannounced in a 'dawn raid'. Dawn raids get press coverage – the authorities like to be seen taking action to tackle corporate misdeeds and will be enthusiastic in informing the media – and you are already in a difficult place as 'there is no smoke without a fire'. The ensuing investigation takes up time and, if you have done something wrong, the fine will hurt. It will also take a lot of time and effort to recover your reputation, and the association itself will find it hard to operate well, as its membership will be loath to be heavily involved and so expose themselves to more problems. The whole thing causes a lot of wreckage in its wake.

WHERE TO FIND FRIENDS

Associations

Associations (organisations representing groups of companies in the same sector) are the most common and easiest way for a company to link up with friends and allies for a political fight.

Even if you are already a member of an association, take a

moment to see if there are other associations active in your political arena. You should also assess if your association(s) are good at lobbying.

A good start is to look at recent press articles about your issue. Which associations are being quoted or referred to? Are any seen as an authority on the subject? Or are they not referred to at all?

You can assess whether an association is proficient at government relations when:

- they provide regular information on what is really happening in political circles on your issue;
- they provide regular opportunities to network with relevant politicians;
- they prepare and approve effective lobbying papers; and
- they follow their papers up with timely meetings with well-targeted politicians.

If the association is reassuring members that all is well because a newsletter has been sent to all parliamentarians, this is not good lobbying. The newsletter will be going straight in politicians' waste paper baskets.

Industry alliances and coalitions
If your existing association is not suitable for your lobbying needs, you should look at forming an alliance or coalition

that is formed to deal with a single issue. Alliances or coalitions are formal groups formed for the specific purpose of advocating on a specific political issue, unlike associations which have a wider role than just lobbying. They vary enormously in their make-up and can include companies, associations, activist groups and think tanks.

Alliances of associations are another option. But it can be difficult. Too often you see a multiplication of bureaucratic systems that slows decision-making, and cultural differences encourage in-fighting and petty politics.

Politicians like meeting with coalitions as they represent a broader field than a single company or sector association. This makes them a useful foundation on which to build a lobbying campaign.

Trade unions

If trade unions are involved in your issue, whether as friends or opponents, they are efficient political players. There is no standard model for how trade unions act or fit into the different political arenas across Europe. They vary enormously from being an official part of the governing institutions, to powerful political powerhouses in 'socialist' regions, to acting like protest groups.

Activists and campaigners

By definition the purpose of an activist is be out there,

actively promoting their causes in the media and political world. Some are well-funded with large memberships and staff, while some have limited resources with no permanent workforce, but all are driven and passionate about their cause.

It is not so easy to team up and cooperate with activist groups. Cultural differences between the corporate and activist worlds are wide, but common ground can be found.

In corporate speak, working with activist groups comes under a 'stakeholder and community outreach' label – an inelegant but accurate description. Mutual suspicion and ignorance best describes the starting point. But when you realise that they are part of the political debate and that they can be very good at lobbying, you would be foolish to ignore them. Mutual cooperation can be highly beneficial for both sides.

They may be weaker on technical knowledge – that is your strength – but they are good politically. Their values and motivations are closer to those of the politicians than companies, giving them an advantage when delivering their messages, and they enjoy a better public and political reputation because they are values-driven.

This does not make them politically bulletproof. If they do things like making exaggerated technical claims, not really representing their supporters' interests or forgetting their values, their reputations can be rapidly damaged. This happened spectacularly with Oxfam, when it emerged that some of its staff were exploiting, not aiding, Haitians recovering from the 2010 earthquake.

Politicians

You often find a group of politicians who have identified themselves as being interested in your issue by being members of semi-official 'parliamentary interest groups'. A good way to find them if you are defeated by official parliamentary websites (notoriously clunky and uninformative) is to look for publicity about charity events and receptions held in the Parliament and find out which parliamentarians spoke at or sponsored the events.

Having a group of interested parliamentarians on your side is a great support. They can give you political advice and help – even if it is just getting you a room to hold an event in their Parliament building.

When I talk about parliamentarians here, I am loosely referring to politicians in all European parliaments. They vary enormously in how they go about their business, but even so, parliamentarians are campaigners by instinct and you should be able to find some interested in your issue.

The media

Getting your message out in the media is an effective way of making your case known, but it can be a double-edged sword: you may not want your story in the papers and if it is about your lobbying activities, it is unlikely to be positive. You may think this view is a bit too downbeat, but it is based on the fact that I have never come across a positive press story about corporate lobbying. A positive story just doesn't cut it. It is much better for journalists to infer underhand or murky dealings in the corridors of power – that sells!

Culturally speaking it is still not seen as 'normal' in Europe that companies actually lobby. Once, when I was working on a climate change issue, a BBC interviewer kicked off by asking me why companies were lobbying at all, as climate change should be discussed only by politicians and climate groups. It was hard to make a good case with that kind of start – I was already the bad guy and I hadn't even opened my mouth.

On the other hand, journalists still need information for their stories and industry can be a good source. You just need to be careful.

Trade journalists are much more likely to take your side as their readership is the industry. They are great if you are trying to drum up support and awareness in your industry, but of no use if you are trying to get heard by politicians who do not read the trade press.

Political journalists – a broad category covering national newspapers, magazines like *The Economist*, *Der Spiegel* and *Time*, TV and radio, and international wires like Reuters and Agence France-Presse (AFP) – are interested in what politicians are doing, especially when there is a good fight going on. They are less interested in technical issues, so when preparing to talk to them, you have to look at your issue from a political angle – what is interesting to their readership?

Too many times industry will bore the journalists because they are not saying anything political. And industry people are frustrated because the journalists are only interested in controversy. Fine if you have gossip to sell, but not if you are talking about cooperation and consensus-building.

In short, do you have a good story to sell to their readership? If not, don't bother.

The Brussels press corps may be the largest in the world, but they must also be the one most bombarded with the longest, most tedious and worst-written press releases on the planet.

Social media

Lobbying and social media are not comfortable bedfellows. Similar to trying to get positive coverage of lobbying, having a Twitter image showing you talking to parliamentarians with a 'great to be lobbying the Parliament today' caption is not a good look.

The best rule of thumb is, if you want to see your tweet in the newspaper the next day, go for it. Otherwise, don't bother.

Local journalists

Local and regional press are unlikely to be enthused about goings on in the national capital or Brussels. Their readership is local and their interest in corporations will be about jobs and new factory buildings. If you are restructuring and jobs are at stake, you need to be talking with them. The unions and local politicians certainly will be.

It makes sense to build a relationship with the local media when positive things are happening. A good combination is to have your local parliamentarian visit, as well as arranging for the local media to be there.

Think tanks and academic institutes

If you want a platform for your issue, think tanks and academic institutes can be very useful, as they can provide third-party endorsement for your arguments and a platform for you to present your case. They vary from semi-academic ones, preoccupied with producing learned papers, to those holding highly political debating sessions.

Consultants

In the political arena, 'consultants' are a diverse range of companies who advise governments and ministries. If a politician wants to find out something, for example whether it is possible to make a more efficient air conditioner or the long-term market trends in electric car sales, they ask consultants. Basically, they provide information and advice on anything a politician does not have the expertise on or time to find out. With many governments and public bodies cutting back on budgets and labour, the number and influence of consultants is growing.

Their influence in the political arena varies enormously depending on the situation. But, as their advice can inform the thinking of how a piece of legislation is designed, they are important to get to know.

Enemies

The cliché 'keep your friends close, but your enemies closer' neatly encapsulates the whole point of knowing and being in contact with all the different political players in your political arena – as they are all potential friends and enemies.

To win a political argument, you need friends, but you also need to know what your opponents are doing and why.

To punch above your weight in the political arena, remember that you will be more influential if you have a good reputation and your voice will be louder if you work well with friends and allies. Know what is going on and who is influential, and always avoid problems with unfair competition rules.

DEALING WITH POLITICAL PROBLEMS AND CRISES

If you run an organisation, politics will find you. Lobbying is about dealing with political risk – challenges, opportunities, problems and crises. Some you will be anticipating, some you identify and some just come your way, driven by the prevailing political winds. But some – the crises – come out of the blue. Good lobbying is about turning political risk into political opportunity.

You may not think you have a political risk – or you may already be losing sleep over one. Either way, political risks are external forces that could harm or help your company.

Political risk comes in many forms. Brexit is probably the biggest political risk currently facing Europe – put simply, a major EU country, the UK, is leaving a free trade area and a common regulatory framework which has determined trading conditions in the European Union for the last forty years. Whatever happens, there will be a big shake up regarding how you do business and how political decisions impact you, regardless of whether you are based in the UK or the EU.

However, there are types of political risk that you may be able to anticipate, for example:

- if you have a breakthrough product or service, but the existing laws are not appropriate or prevent you going to market;
- if you need political support, but no one knows you and you don't know any politicians;
- if you need funding (e.g. for a factory modernisation or a new roundabout to ease congestion at your site);
- if you want to restructure your business and look at re-tooling and training your workforce but need help (i.e. public money) to keep your costs competitive;
- laws are being discussed that might ban or phase out your products; or
- an agency does not approve your product, or actively wants it off the market.

You might believe that your products and services are politically future proof, but consider leaded petrol, cigarettes, foam hamburger boxes, lead solder, some fridges, noisy aircraft, cars without airbags, filament light bulbs and coal-burning power stations. Admittedly most of these things are unlamented, but they were legal and profitable until politicians decided to stop or curb them. Many companies probably suffered financially if they did not anticipate these political challenges, but the smart ones profited.

Sometimes the politicians knew what they were doing and what this would cost, and sometimes they did not (or did not care).

Often in politics your industry or product just gets picked on, so you always need to be aware of how the political wind is blowing in order to see it coming. When it blows in your direction, you will need to be engaging with politicians. Otherwise, without knowing it, you will end up being the target, or just the collateral damage, of political action.

The infamous American gangster Al Capone reputedly summed up the situation succinctly: 'You're either at the table, or on the menu.'

The car industry's failure to anticipate the political drive towards recycling is an instructive case of a usually politically savvy industry failing to be at the right political table at the right time. They were blown over by recycling politics and paid the price.

In the 1990s, there was a growing realisation that the ever-increasing use of natural resources and the dumping of waste in landfill – the 'throw-away culture' – could not go on for ever. The solution was to persuade everyone to recycle.

The biggest sources of waste are governments, construction

and food, and the largest problem is plastics, as they have so little economic value after their use and they can take centuries to biodegrade.

However, a car is mainly made of metal, is often repaired to extend its life, often has many owners and, when it is too old to drive, there is a recycling industry which is happy to dismantle it and recycle the metals. It is in fact the most highly reused and recycled consumer product and one that is hardly ever just thrown away.

If you wanted to push and promote recycling, you would have thought one would aim at single-use products. However, politicians took steady aim at cars, because they had the highest public profile among consumer products. The political thinking went that if you made an example of cars, this would then encourage the whole of society to recycle more.

The car industry, facing complex and costly recycling legislation, was dumbfounded and could not understand why its arguments – that cars amounted to less than 2 per cent of waste going to landfill – were being ignored. Further, the politicians said that the carmakers should be responsible for the whole life of their products – taking the new concept of 'extended producer responsibility' from Sweden – in order to make sure cars were recycled. Industry arguments that drivers should be responsible for their cars and that, in any case, a car recycling industry already existed, cut no ice at all. EU rules were agreed on that gave drivers the right to take their cars to car dealers for recycling with no charge.

Governments wanted the carmakers to be seen to be made financially responsible for recycling cars and, at the same time, did not want to impose any costs on car owners – mainly because they are also voters.

At the same time, a law was being drafted to impose similar recycling responsibilities on construction waste, but when it was realised that the major construction waste producers were the governments themselves, the draft law was discreetly left to gather dust in a forgotten drawer.

There are several important take-aways with this story:

- Carmakers and recyclers failed to be at the table at the right time and were written firmly into the political menu.
- Voters are more important to politicians than industry, even large ones like the car industry.
- Politicians assume industry can afford the impositions and costs of legislation – in fact, they often assume they are doing the right thing when industry complains loudly.
- Corporations are not popular and make tempting targets for politicians.
- It is easy for politicians to paint industry as the bad guys in resisting progress or environmental improvements.
- Voters do not mind if industry is seen to be taking on the costs of laws.

To counter these attitudes, industry needs to be sophisticated when putting together its arguments. Being in denial, or arguing that you are not the real problem and that laws will be hugely expensive, will not get you far. Raising the spectre of job losses is tempting and can work if properly done with solid facts and figures, but unfortunately it has been used so often that now few politicians really believe it.

So when you are in the political crosshairs, it is much better to accept it, analyse the situation and come up with a better alternative to achieve your political aim. A good way is to look for a collaborative approach to politicians, rather than an antagonistic one which is unlikely to work very well. Obstruction and protest all the way up the political ladder to the German Chancellor did not work out for the carmakers.

They should have seen the recycling issue coming their way. They failed to, as they failed to see that many politicians saw cars as a societal problem, not as an unalloyed benefit.

To avoid making the same mistake, it is a good idea to be aware of what is driving politicians. It is generally: safety, the environment, privacy and security. These are four powerful words and four powerful reasons for why politicians are moved to act.

When you are analysing your situation, you need to ask what is motivating the politicians involved? Are they saying that their policies will make voters safer, safeguard the planet for future generations, protect society from social media manipulation or protect jobs?

These are strong vote winners. Which minister would not want to act to make people safer? If your counter arguments are that such-and-such a policy is ill-directed, ill-designed, expensive and will cost jobs, you are probably entering a losing battle. What you need to do is study these motivations and use them as your starting point when forming your counter arguments, which will immediately make them politically relevant.

Say you are a lift manufacturer and your workforce is having problems mending ancient technologies in old lifts, when you would much prefer to be making money selling new lifts. What you should not do is argue for laws to impose costly lift modernisations on building owners to keep your workers safe. The minister will hardly listen to you before showing you the door. Instead, you need to argue that modern lifts are needed so that everyone in society can use them safely. The minister is now much more likely to listen to you, as the motivator of public safety is at stake, not your financial interests. You will also be more able to get others to support your cause.

Take another example of green or health taxes. They are politically popular, as who would want to oppose a green tax, or indeed a health tax on sugar, especially when it is corporations that will pay it directly? It is hard to get popular sympathy for your plight.

In principle the tax may be impossible to resist, but you can ask where the tax revenues are going. Government treasuries love raising tax income, but hate having their hands bound as to where the tax money is eventually spent. The tax may be green or healthy, but they do not want the environment ministry to have the right to spend it. So your best bet would be to talk to the Treasury, and argue that it is a bad tax as it can be easily avoided, encourage crime, hurt exports and render less tax than its supporters claim. All good reasons, as far as the Treasury is concerned, to water down green and health taxes.

New technologies inspire inventors and excite engineers and companies, but they can easily worry politicians and the public. Just think about the dystopian imagery of the *Terminator* films, or indeed in any film where intelligent machines go wrong.

The ability to work with things at a startlingly small scale (e.g. nanotechnology) is exciting. When informing a series of European parliamentarians about nanotechnology, companies were expecting reactions of excitement and curiosity about this coming revolution, but this was not the case. Instead, they found parliamentarians who had no idea what nanotechnology was, but nevertheless wanted to ban it, because it just sounded bad to them.

This fear of the new is encapsulated in the 'precautionary principle', which has actually been written into EU statutes. The principle sets out that if there is the possibility of exposure to harm, decisions will not be made where extensive scientific knowledge is lacking. Or in simpler terms, politicians will only support something if it is risk-free for the public or the environment.

In theory, who could argue with that? But in the real world, extensive scientific data does not exist for new technologies – for example, fracking, nanotechnology, GMOs and new chemicals – and you would be asking politicians to take a huge risk in supporting them. This is a tricky job, as saying no is always easier than saying yes for a politician.

The difficulty is that all chemicals and technologies pose some sort of risk. A bullet is obviously hazardous, but do you ban all bullets to make the world safe, or do you manage their risks to make them safe? As risk management is so nuanced, politicians are less attracted to it and you will need to be convincing.

Chemicals have a history of being attacked and distrusted. 'Chemicals' was a sexy term from the industrial revolution until the 1980s, when they went from being poster boys of technological advancement to being synonymous with 'poison'. 'Synthetic' no longer meant modern, rather non-natural and probably toxic.

Arguments about new and future chemicals rage in political circles. The chemical industry has been slow to realise that it was no longer attractive. Meanwhile, officials and politicians were slow to realise that everything can be hazardous and you cannot just ban everything.

The precautionary principle has put a dampener on research and innovation in Europe, but it has also pushed industry into taking social and political concerns seriously. If you fail to do so, you will never develop the politically telling arguments needed to win your case.

DIESEL-GATE AND THE BREAKDOWN OF TRUST

Credibility and a good reputation are so important. If you lose it, politicians won't believe what you are saying and will be reluctant to take your side in a political battle. Diesel-gate is a classic case of a breakdown of credibility and reputation.

Business had been repeatedly accused of 'greenwashing' – varying from allegations for making groundless or exaggerated claims for the environmental advantages of a business, to simply making their marketing and commercials look greener. But, on the whole, greenwashing accusations were allegations, not proven facts.

Now after two decades of environmental laws and spreading environmental and energy efficiency standards, it is no longer the Wild West for making green claims. Industries have to meet environmental standards before they can crow about the environmental benefits of products to customers.

Game over for the greenwashers then? No. A few years ago, a car manufacturer ran a bus straight through the validity and public confidence in environmental standards when they allegedly gamed the standard-setting test procedures, in order for their diesel engines to ostensibly meet the standards.

This was a big political and reputational problem. The company, and indeed the whole car industry, became the target of political ire – but it also smeared the reputation for all businesses. Claims of meeting standards are looked at askance and industry calls for better-designed regulations fall on suspicious political ears.

The negative impact of diesel-gate on the reputation of industry will be far reaching and long-lasting. Businesses are looking keenly at competing in the world of Big Data and smart machines to revolutionise product performance and productivity – whether that is prescribing medicines or maintaining electric turbines in power stations. And there will be suspicions about what industry is doing with all this data they are gathering. Politicians will not be satisfied with a 'trust us' stance from industry. They will want to regulate, and having your reputation damaged in advance already puts you on the back foot when trying to make your case.

FEAR OF THE FUTURE

Fear of the new does not just raise its head in the environmental field. Artificial Intelligence and Big Data hold enormous promise to change people's lives for the better. However, regulators are worried, sometimes justifiably, about how it will give companies the ability to constantly keep people under surveillance and manipulate them – from gaming price comparison sites to decreasing lending limits for couples if marriage guidance counselling bills appear on their credit card bills, as has happened in the US.

As the chair of the UK Financial Conduct Authority, Charles Randell, suggested in July 2018, regulation is central in making sure new technology (in the finance sector) remains a force for good and keeps people free to make well-informed decisions. He described the danger of a dystopian future where there is neither a democracy where citizens decide, nor a bureaucracy where officials like him decide, but instead an 'algocracy' where algorithms decide.

He made these comments just a day after Facebook was fined £500,000 for failing to protect users' data in the UK, which was used by Cambridge Analytica for targeted political advertising.

Arguments about personal data and data privacy will continue. Social media firms have been surprised by their rapid descent from the golden boys of the modern internet and social interaction (e.g. the shared economy and the gig economy) to the bad guys exploiting data for their own gain and endangering democracy with voter profiling.

To win political battles here, social media firms have to deal with the public fears over the misuse of data. Unless they do so, they risk seeing their good reputation declining and being buried in rules that could weaken their businesses. Political views on data privacy are very different on either side of the Atlantic. They may still be heroes in the US and Silicon Valley, which eases their US regulatory burden, but they are not the golden boys in Europe – they are the outsiders.

GETTING ON SIDE

Politicians everywhere want to help their 'home' team. If you are a French company trying to win an argument in Germany, you could appeal to European solidarity to support your case. It could still be an option if you are Swiss, but if you are

American, Indian, Chinese or Japanese you have to make a real effort to be seen as a friend and not the outsider.

If you are in this situation, referring to how much better your domestic legislation or policies are is an absolute no-no. It will only come across as arrogance – even if you're right.

The best argument you can use to get on side is your employee numbers in Europe, or specifically in the country in which you are meeting the politicians. Export percentages are good too, as they are earning the country money. Your earnings are not really relevant as your shareholders are outside Europe, and it brings up the question of how much tax you are paying. This is a negative line of discussion you do not want to pursue, but have to be prepared for if asked. It is also good to be part of a European or national alliance or association, or working with NGOs.

Your aim is to show that you are one of them and share their concerns, which is the first step towards building a rapport. Without a rapport you are going nowhere fast.

I have gone into some detail here on the fears and concerns that drive politicians, as well as some of the events that have shaped the reputation of industry in political circles. I might have been a bit bleak in drawing the scenery, but this was on purpose. People own, run and work in companies that they believe are doing the right thing with the right technologies – carmakers see cars as wonderful and social media companies see data as the future. It is the same across all businesses whether you are making medicines, running restaurants or building railways. What I have tried to get across is that society and politicians do not always see your business in the same light as you do. They have fears that may seem illogical, misguided or misinformed, but when you are lobbying and forming your arguments you have to take these fears and lack of knowledge totally on board and tackle them head on. Then you can not only be at the right table, at the right time, but you also can speak the right way in order to allay their fears, build up a rapport and win your arguments.

CRISIS MANAGEMENT

The next political problem that may come your way is the political crisis – when you are being shot at by politicians. When that happens, you need to move quickly and have a plan to get yourself out of the firing line.

In a phrase, crisis management is about hoping for the best and preparing for the worst.

Unless you are actually planning to create a crisis, it is an unexpected, nasty, fast-moving event that puts the reputation, financial health and even existence of your company at risk.

There are many examples of a crisis: an oil spill or environmental disaster, the crashing of an online banking system, workers demonstrating about a plant closure, a major data breach, the fatality of a worker, a fatal fire in a supplier's factory, faulty medical implants, the discovery that suppliers are using slave labour, the leaking of trade secrets to a foreign power, faulty products on the market that are endangering people, a terrorist attack, company misdeeds like cartels... the list goes on.

The common factor is that something has happened to a business that you directly or indirectly control or are responsible for, and it has gone horribly wrong.

What matters is how you react to the problem – the clock is ticking and there are a lot of upset people. Get it wrong and your company stands to lose its reputation and indeed its very existence.

You and your people need to be able to work at speed and react under pressure, as the first hours of a crisis are the most critical in fixing the perception (although not necessarily the reality) of a crisis and the company involved. The period of crisis is chaotic and fast-moving, and it is definitely not the time to be figuring out plans, sorting out principles of action or putting structures and people into place.

The leadership of the company will be under a lot of public scrutiny. How the leadership reacts in a crisis is a telling indicator of the quality of management and the basic values of the company.

Perception is all-important and the public and politicians will be expecting a human or empathic reaction from the company. Legalese, obfuscation and blame-laying are never attractive and will turn perceptions against you. What you want to emerge is your company's solid values, and this means sticking to them and communicating openly and consistently.

An advisor of President Clinton had good advice: 'Tell it early. Tell it all. Tell it yourself.'

If politicians hate to hear about job losses, they hate surprises even more. Once, the CEO of a US corporation met the French President on a Thursday, saying that all was well with its operations in France; the following Monday, they announced big lay-offs. The Élysée Palace was infuriated not to get any advance warning and the reputation of the US company took a big hit from the people who really matter politically in France. Not a good move. The company should have been prepared to tell the bad news, even if it might have been difficult for their CEO.

PLANNING AND PREPARATION

You need a plan.

As far as the political side of things are concerned, you need to categorise politicians as a stakeholder group in your planning, alongside the other groups you have to communicate with – customers, employees, investors, the media, social and environmental activists, and trade unions.

Companies are usually well set up for talking with employees and their local media and trade press. But are you ready for the national press, TV camera crews and a viral story on social media, all the while coping with denunciations from trade unions, activists, parliamentarians and ministers? When you are briefing your workers you may be behind doors – but remember that everybody's phone is a video camera now. How will the briefing go down on social media?

When planning politically, you must ensure you know the local MPs, not just where your factory or office buildings are, but also where your employees live, as well as whom to contact in the ministry that mainly covers your area of business.

A political crisis checklist should include:

1. Who are the core crisis management group members?
2. Who will be the company spokespeople (i.e. who can talk to external stakeholders)?
3. Have all spokespeople received media training?
4. Do people in the company know who to contact in a crisis?
5. Does everyone in the company know who their spokespeople are? (You do not want an unplanned company comment in the media.)
6. Who will prepare a holding statement and who will comment and approve it? And by when?
7. Who will decide how to respond to questions from politicians?
8. Will the group in principle agree to meet politicians?
9. Will the group in principle agree to attend a parliamentary committee?
10. If everyone in the core group is not available, what is

the minimum group that have the authority to prepare and approve a public comment? It is best to meet face to face or, failing that, in a conference call. Emailing is not quick, nor secure enough.

11.   Which politicians have to be contacted personally at local, regional and national levels?

12.   Who will make the actual calls?

13.   Which politicians and other external stakeholders can be informed by email?

14.   What is the timescale for contacting all key external stakeholders? It should be a matter of hours, as you do not have days.

15.   Who will actually meet the ministers, local MPs and mayors?

16.   Who will organise telephone numbers and email addresses?

A decision has to be made in principle to agree to meet with and communicate with politicians. This is important, as it creates the right mind-set – we are going to communicate and we need to plan for it. Not taking a decision on a communication policy can encourage the avoidance of active communication and foster a bunker mentality. In turn, a bunker mentality leads to groupthink, which lacks perspective, proportion or empathy with external stakeholders in the unfolding crisis.

Saying nothing is not a realistic option. If you are silent, your opponents and critics will do all the talking and you will have no voice or influence in the political debate.

'Out of touch', 'insensitive', 'arrogant', 'unresponsive' are all adjectives you do not want to be labelled with during a crisis, as are 'panicky', 'disorganised' and 'indecisive'.

So, your group, policy and systems have to be tested and practised. You do not want to be going through a crisis with an untested system.

When you practise, make sure that the senior leadership are directly involved. In a crisis, the leadership will be the key decision makers and spokespeople for the company, so they need to be familiar with the crisis management system and the people involved. They are also probably the people who will have to sign off on holding statements and give the go-ahead to contact external shareholders. If 'practice and rehearsal' sound too boring, call it 'war gaming'.

Are you and your team ready? If you have practised for an aggressive media interview during media training, have you also practised for a tricky political meeting?

If the outreach results in a politician wanting to visit your offices or factory accompanied by the media, do you know where you will allow the cameras to film? Where do you put the media when they arrive? These are all practical issues that ideally need to be resolved in advance.

Will you let the media interview workers on site? Will you let a politician have a televised question and answer session with your workforce? You have to assume that it will not only be the media filming. Everyone with a smartphone can film it and post it on the internet.

It goes without saying that war gaming has to be as realistic as possible to really test your system and see if it works. A well-drilled team will operate efficiently under pressure.

Hopefully you will never need to use a crisis plan, but just having one gives people confidence that the company can cope and survive in a crisis.

HOW NOT TO DEAL WITH A POLITICAL CRISIS

Politics can seem a distant world from a company's everyday concerns and activities, especially when dealing with a foreign country. However, this is a mistake. Get on the wrong side of politicians and life can get pretty uncomfortable, pretty fast.

In 2010, Kraft gave an object lesson in not only creating its own crisis, but then making it worse when the political sparks began to fly.

Kraft is a large US multinational in the food business which was looking to grow its market share by buying Cadbury, a famous British chocolate maker. Kraft launched its hostile bid in 2009 and it was headline news in the UK, as the Cadbury brand was much loved.

During the negotiations, the then UK Business Secretary, Lord Mandelson, said that the government would not approve any buyer of Cadbury that failed to respect the historic confectioner. Kraft responded by stating that the UK would be a net beneficiary of jobs and specifically promised that it would continue to operate a particular factory that had been under some pressure.

The CEO of Kraft even met Mandelson on 2 February 2010 when Kraft's bid succeeded – repeating public pledges to keep the factory open and restating what she had said in an email to the minister, that the takeover would be good news for British manufacturing and that it was expected to create jobs.

But then the wheels came off. A mere seven days later, Kraft said that it was going to close the factory, resulting in the loss of 400 employees.

Consequently, the company should have anticipated the impending levels of political discomfort that lay in store for it, depending how it played its hand:

1. A letter or quote of a parliamentarian in the local press attacking the company.
2. Questions asked in Parliament or calls for a debate.
3. Criticism in a parliamentary debate (for which you cannot sue for libel).
4. Being summoned before a parliamentary committee.
5. Ministerial criticism.
6. Trade union criticism (which was influential, given that the socialist Labour Party was in power).
7. A parliamentary inquiry.
8. Sanctions from the UK Takeover Panel, the regulatory

agency for making misleading statements of intent before the deal.

9. Punitive fines.

Eventually, Kraft escaped the fines and received only an embarrassing formal public criticism from the Takeover Panel in May 2010. Nevertheless, it went through all the other levels of political discomfort and its reputation in the UK was thus permanently damaged.

Of course, Kraft's biggest mistake was making pledges about jobs and future manufacturing plans that it kept only for seven days – but then it started digging a deeper hole for itself.

The company failed to apologise or show any remorse for making misleading public statements, to sympathise with its workers or give politicians a heads up on its intentions. Then, as the political furore continued unabated, its CEO famously failed to turn up in person to represent Kraft at a parliamentary committee hearing, leaving lower-level executives to take the political heat.

It instead tried to say, unconvincingly, that its commercial decision to close the factory was made only when it became aware of the facts after it actually signed the deal, and that it was merely upholding the closure plans already made by Cadbury. Did it really think that it could avoid criticism by claiming ignorance and placing the blame on the previous management?

It also tried to spin the 'difficult' decision to close the factory as a good one for the workers, as it had moved quickly to remove any uncertainty about their future.

However, Kraft received public criticism from the Prime Minister and the trade minister, angry headlines and parliamentarians accusing it of 'irresponsible' and 'cynical' behaviour, 'arrogance' and acting like 'Vikings' asset stripping the UK industry.

Eventually, the company was dragged unwillingly before a parliamentary committee and forced to apologise, admitting at the hearing that 'reputations are fragile' – a classic piece of masterly understatement.

Kraft may have bought Cadbury and it may have escaped punitive fines, but its reputation lay in tatters.

What this story illustrates is that Kraft's decision makers were clearly in their own bubble. They appeared to have lost the ability to judge how their decisions would be seen in the UK, and lacked political awareness. Even when the storm broke, they did not alter their behaviour to mitigate the fallout. It was not just a failure to appreciate the strength of feeling towards Cadbury as an iconic brand, but also to adapt when things went badly.

This is a painful example of a company getting its crisis management completely wrong and paying a heavy political price for it.

Finding yourself in the political crosshairs is truly an uncomfortable place to be. In order to avoid getting yourself in this position you have to keep in mind that politics can always find you, that political risks are real and that it is not a sensible strategy just to ignore politics. If your industry and technologies are getting bad press, take it seriously and do not just brush it off as uninformed and biased. Take time to understand why you are being critiqued and remember that politicians care more about voters than companies. Finally, be proactive in putting plans and structures into place so your company is ready to respond to a crisis if it happens.

—

PERSUASIVE UNDER PRESSURE

To really make an impact when lobbying, you need to meet the politicians face to face. It is usually on their ground, rarely comfortable and you still have to make your case – it's all about being persuasive under pressure.

The first essential is to get your communication right. Second, you must polish your persuasion techniques, including having a contingency for what to do if the meeting goes all wrong. Then comes the actual planning of the meeting, where you ensure that as much as possible is set up in your favour in advance. And, finally, you will need to gear yourself up for the meeting and ensure your body language is spot on.

COMMUNICATION

ARE YOU SHOUTING LOUD ENOUGH?

The old-fashioned joke goes that if you are trying to communicate with someone abroad, you speak in your own language and if you do not succeed at first, you just repeat it louder. That should do the trick, right?

No – but it does describe how many people go about their lobbying.

Other descriptions that come to mind are 'a dialogue of the deaf' and the oft-heard complaint in industry circles that politicians and other players like NGOs and the media unfairly use emotional arguments, while industry has to stick to facts, correct terminology and properly detailed arguments.

These three faults – plain arrogance, the refusal to adapt one's approach and the failure to understand why the political world cannot appreciate 'your language' – are very common and are the root cause for so many campaigns running into the sand.

One tempting solution in these times of demagogues and rabble-rousing politicians is to use 'alternative facts' and to denounce all opposing arguments as 'fake news'. But that would not be responsible or effective, and your good reputation would rapidly disappear.

What doesn't work

1.   Insisting on using industry jargon.

2. Hyperbole.
3. Including all your detailed arguments and facts in your speeches, press releases and conversations.
4. Assuming that your political audience will want to wade through all your lovingly prepared policy papers because that 'is their job'.

What does work

1. Using simple, plain language.
2. Keeping it short – who can remember more than three key points?
3. Using a clear structure.

Using industry terminology will probably seem sensible as the terms are correct and exact, and you use them every day. However, they should not be used during a lobbying meeting, for two big reasons: those from outside your industry will not understand the jargon, and it will make them feel like they are outsiders when they listen to you. You will have definitely failed to strike up a rapport with your audience. At the same time, using political jargon in your speeches and press releases is not a good idea either, for the same reasons – why should your audience care about your message if it only exists in a nebulous distant political world which they are excluded from, and why should they learn the political terms so that they can actually understand what your problem is?

Have a look at your typical industry magazine – it will be

overflowing with industry jargon and acronyms. They use this language as it is inclusive – its readers are more likely to feel involved and special, but the chances that the general reader will read, let alone buy, the magazine are incredibly low. When you lobby, your communications cannot sound as though they have come out of an industry magazine.

It can be disheartening and sometimes painfully amusing to hear or read about a political debate in which business talked about 'units' when they meant cars, 'buildings' when they should have said homes and offices; and political jargon like 'draft directives' and 'rapporteurs' when they meant new laws and parliamentary committee reporters.

Keeping it simple can be a tricky process – adding complexity is easy, particularly when groups of people are involved. Saying 'Industry is supporting efforts by the European Commission to improve the energy efficiency of building envelopes' may be correct, but besides being boring, it is complex, uses jargon and leaves one cold. It would be much better to say 'We want lower heating bills.' There is no jargon, it's inclusive (as everyone lives in a home with heating) and it's simple.

Hyperbole sounds great, is positive and gets noticed – but can you back it up with facts? How many times do you hear that a policy will mean thousands of job losses and the collapse of business as we know it? Statistical hyperbole in the form of extrapolating trends is a curse (you will hear that 'based on current trends' a certain industry will disappear, endanger the planet or cause irreparable harm, for example) – but trends never do keep going in one direction. This is speculation at best, or just plain exaggeration designed to spin an argument.

Similarly, keeping it short is tricky when you really want to bring all your arguments and facts to bear. It is best to see the challenge in terms of a friendly conversation. You can't have a good conversation with someone if you are just speaking at them, hoping that they will stay attentive before they find a polite excuse to talk to someone else. I have to admit here that at one lobbying meeting, a colleague was going into such endless detail with a politician that I nodded off. Luckily, I woke up before they noticed (or they were too polite to tease me about it). As with your initial strategy, a 'rule of three' is useful here. Use your three key points (no cheating by adding sub-points) and keep to them.

You must also keep it interesting. What makes for a good story? A great introduction, well-plotted story lines, drama, laughter, energy, snappy language, intriguing characters and villains, memorable lines, suspense and a neat ending. A great way to add drama and make your argument memorable is to bring along your product. If it is too large, bring a model. If this is not possible, bring a picture.

You might not be able to get all these ingredients in, but the essentials – structure and energy – will mean you are not left trying to sell a boring story. You will be more convincing and interesting.

In terms of structure, Aristotle said an argument should have two parts: the first sets out the points at issue; and the second makes the case. This is a good basis, but there is a more developed, six-part structure:

1. Introduction.
2. Narration – set out the established facts.
3. Division – set out the points at issue.
4. Proof – make your case.
5. Refutation – demolish the opponent's case.
6. Sum up.

In other words, you should tell your audience what you are going to say, say it and then tell them what you said.

When summing up, the most important thing to do is finish with your strongest point, as the last thing your audience hears will leave the strongest impression. It is not for nothing that bands play their big hits in the encore and not at the start of the concert.

Finally, a word on language. If you are a native English speaker, you are in a lucky position, as nearly all the politicians in Brussels and many in the capital cities of Europe speak English, and often very well at that. Nevertheless, you have to remember that it is not their first language, so stay away from colloquialisms and slang, and finish your sentences. You may not realise it, but in everyday conversations the English often leave their sentences unfinished, as they assume everyone around them knows how the sentence will end. But non-English officials will not necessarily know.

I heard of a wonderful example of someone getting the wrong end of the stick because of English language usage. A lobbyist was putting forward a contentious point, when the Commission official said that he was 'astonished' she had brought it up. Afterwards, the lobbyist was very pleased that her point had been so well received, as the official had been 'astonished'. She had to be let down gently that she had just received a criticism, not a compliment, from the official.

PREPARING FOR THE MEETING

WHY DO MEETINGS?

A lot of this book is focused on preparing for face-to-face meetings, as this is the most effective way to get your argument across to the right people, at the right time and in the right way. Even if your strategy is focused on public campaigning, press events and conferences, you still need to be able to secure and perform well in meetings. If you are doing so, you will probably find that the rest of the campaign is well-targeted and set in the right tone.

Targeting is the critical first step: meet the right people, at the right time.

SETTING UP THE MEETING IN YOUR FAVOUR

Generally there are two types of meeting: a networking or a 'get-to-know' meeting; or a lobbying or a 'we need to get our point across and persuade' meeting. Either way, the organisation and preparation are basically the same.

First ask yourself, why should this politician want or need to meet me? When you call or email their office, you need a twenty-second elevator pitch or single paragraph summarising why you think the politician should meet you. When you have successfully done that, send a follow-up email restating why you want the meeting, who you are, who will be attending the meeting from your side and confirming or asking for a meeting date and time.

In subsequent correspondence and telephone calls with the politician's office, you should reiterate the outline of the points or subjects you plan to bring up and ask if there are specific points that they are likely to mention. This is stage management, and ensures both that the politician is properly briefed by their officials and thus more comfortable that the meeting will contain no surprises, and that you are equally well-prepared.

Here is an example of a typical request note:

We heard your minister talking at a conference recently and are very pleased that she is taking a keen interest in x issue. We are experts in x issue and represent the wider industry on this matter. The industry leadership would like to have the opportunity to meet the minister and brief her on the latest technological solutions and the opportunities we see in creating jobs and attracting investment. We hope that a suitable date can be found in her diary in the coming month.

This note shows that: you are aware that the issue is live for the minister and the ministry; you know what the minister is saying; you are offering to provide expert and high-level information from an important group on solutions to the issue; and you come with the promise of new jobs and investment. These are all good reasons why the minister and officials should take notice and agree to see you.

PREPARATION IS EVERYTHING

When you go into a meeting with a politician, whether it is a Prime Minister or a junior official, it will always go better if you are well-prepared. You can then walk into the ministry building with calm and equanimity.

Whether you memorise everything or prefer a briefing book, I favour a two-page brief. The first page has all the details of the meeting and on the second page the photo and biography of the person you are meeting. A photo on the front page is OK, but not a good idea if you aim to put the paper on the table before you – the person you are meeting may find it incongruous or off-putting to be looking down at a photo of themselves while talking with you.

In the next section we will go into the detail of preparing

yourself and your arguments – but here we start with the checklist of essentials that you need to go through before you walk into that building.

Who is attending?

In advance, confirm who will be coming to the meeting and ask if there are any biographical details available. If you are going to see a minister, they will definitely have a biography available, or you will be able to find one on Wikipedia or the ministry website. Officials are less likely to have an official biography, but you can try to see if they are on social media.

Researching the attendees is useful as it can give you an initial feel for the person you are going to meet and help you prepare for how you are going to put your points across. Did they work outside politics before? Are they from an academic background or a trade unionist? What are their main interests or what issues do they champion? If they are a parliamentarian, what issues are featured on their constituency website and have they been quoted in the local press?

You should also be ready to send them your biography and photo. If they do not ask for it, offer it anyway.

It is also best to confirm who will be your contact on the day of the meeting and their telephone number, in case of delays or last-minute changes.

Venue and timing

Know where you are going. Pretty basic I know, but ministries can have many large buildings and different entry points. Inevitably, they are never close together, nor easy to get to if you have turned up at the wrong place. When it goes wrong, it always seems to rain, adding misery to the whole process of finding the right door! To add a further complexity, ministers in the UK have two offices – one in their ministry and one in the Houses of Parliament. Therefore, always double check the address and the entry point.

Sadly, security procedures are part of everyday life and it is the norm that you should expect security similar to an airport when you arrive.

Once you are through, you will either be met or you will need to register at the front desk for them to ring up to the office. Many of the old ministry buildings have no lifts, so expect a bit of a trek upstairs and along endless corridors.

You do not want to be doing any of this in a hurry. Parliaments can be a bit of a zoo at peak times – first thing in the morning, after lunch and early evening – with masses of people turning up for meetings, committee sessions and receptions, as well as being often plagued by slow security and cumbersome registration procedures, it can take an age to get through. Arriving thirty minutes beforehand is a good idea.

Protocol

If you are meeting a minister, a senior civil servant, ambassador or a higher-level personage like a Prime Minister, you need to check how you should address them. If they have a title, like 'Sir' or 'Dame' in the UK, just check beforehand how you like to be addressed. Some will wave the title away, responding, 'Please, just call me John'; others you will have to keep calling 'Sir John'.

In the UK it is mostly the same with 'minister' – after the first time, the usual response is, 'Please, just call me Jane,' so you rapidly go from the formal to the informal.

Elsewhere in Europe, the level of formality is usually retained. In countries like Germany, Austria, Spain and France, I have always used 'minister' and have never been invited to address the minister informally.

Your briefing paper (or cheat sheet)
Prepare a briefing paper that contains the following essential details for the meeting:

- your main message and key supporting points;
- your 'ask';
- key background information on your company or association, such as employee numbers and factory locations; and
- biographical details of the attendees.

Your ask
What is your key ask? This could be asking for the politician's active support to visit a factory, speak at a conference, table

an amendment, or ask a formal parliamentary question? Whatever it is, you need one. If you do not bring it up, the politician will undoubtedly ask, 'How can I help you?' or 'What do you want from me?' and you need an answer.

I have found that putting all the necessary information on two pages gives focus to the briefing and the planning, and it can be easily remembered.

One time, I had to help brief a very senior Japanese corporate representative before their meeting with a minister. The corporate office had painstakingly produced a sixty-five page briefing folder, which included twenty pages of possible questions and answers. After the meeting I asked the translator, who was the only third party present, 'How did the meeting go? Did he make his points and present his ask?' The translator looked uncomfortable for a moment, before smiling and replying, 'They enjoyed chatting about a Japanese novelist and did not talk about business or politics at all!' Afterwards, I could put a positive spin on it that at least the meeting had happened and it was friendly, so all was not lost. But even so, it had achieved nothing concrete and the sixty-five page briefing paper went into the bin – where it should have gone in the first place.

A leave-behind
A 'leave-behind' is literally that – a brochure, presentation, position paper, model, book or memory chip that is left behind with the politician.

Ideally, it will summarise your points and key data in a short format that is easy to read, using good imagery and brevity. Often the leave-behind is the actual document you have been using as a prop during the meeting.

The question is, do they have an impact?

It is hard to tell, really, so I trust to practicality. Is it easy for the officials to slip into a file? Is it amusing enough to keep on the desk? I have seen some clever ornament-like objects, as well as some well-made desk calendars, that have been left behind and have actually stayed on the minister's desk.

During one campaign on renewable energy, I kept coming across good-quality, quite large models of wind turbines in officials' and ministers' offices as I was doing the rounds. The very fact they were there on show made them good leave-behinds – you can be quite innovative and creative. A really creative and memorable one was made by an environmental group who left fluffy toy monkeys hanging off the doorknobs of European parliamentarians' offices to make their point.

A thank-you note

Some people may think this old-fashioned, but a thank-you note is a powerful way to make people feel good. Tell them how valuable the meeting was to you and how appreciative you were that they spared their time to see you.

It is always easier if you do this quickly after the meeting – then you do not have to cover every point and agreed action.

You can always get back to them later, but the important thing is to get your thank-you note out quickly.

People remember a swift note of thanks and will appreciate it, and when you need to see them again they will be better predisposed to you and your request.

All these preparations should ensure that you are entering the building with equanimity. Next, you will need to play your role to maximum effect in the meeting itself, and that depends a lot on how your body is talking.

BODY LANGUAGE

MAKING YOUR PRESENCE FELT

When you meet and talk to people, it is your body that is doing most of the talking and making most of the impact. The importance of body language should never be underestimated and you need to be aware of this fact and make it work for you.

Some studies have indicated that a speaker's words can amount to less than 10 per cent of their overall impact. It is the tone of their voice, together with body position, facial expressions, hand gestures and other non-verbal signs that make up the rest.

Making a good first impression is important for a successful meeting. Whatever the exact percentages of speaker impact may be, the critical take-away here is that if you are not aware or making the most of your body language, you are making your life harder and losing an advantage.

People are most persuaded by those who look and sound confident, likeable and trustworthy. In a word, you need presence.

Politicians are a tough audience to persuade and as soon as you come into view, it is your body that is communicating. When you start speaking, it is the tone of your voice which is more telling than what you are actually saying and it is your body that is giving out the key signals that you are interested, engaged and open.

The good news is that you can practise and improve on this. Most of the emphasis in preparing for a meeting – your typical run-through with colleagues and in corporate training – is focused on structure and presenting key points. This is all well and good, but you also need to focus on how you will come across – you muck this up and your painstakingly crafted points will fail to make an impact.

At the end of the day, humans are animals – an obvious point, but try looking at a political meeting from the perspective of animal behaviour.

You are the stranger accompanied by your pack, invading the space of another pack. Overly aggressive or overly timid, you will be triggering flight or fight responses, combined with territorial protectiveness. These instinctive responses immediately close the minds of your audience from actively listening to you, as you have either established yourself as a threat or someone who can be safely ignored. You need to make yourself a welcome and significant addition to the meeting room, or pack space.

You must work to set everyone at ease as rapidly as possible, by not invading their space, disturbing their pack hierarchy or being a threat.

A perfect illustration of this was a scene in the TV programme *Sherlock*. The arch-villain enters Sherlock and Watson's study and promptly starts by sitting uninvited in Sherlock's chair. He then gets up, stands very close to Sherlock and invades his personal space, touching his face and, as a finale, turns around to pee in his fireplace.

It made great drama precisely because the villain broke so many of the unspoken rules of civil behaviour when in someone else's space. I cannot remember what the villain said, but I certainly remember his actions.

I have put together some tips to avoid the pitfalls and pratfalls of meeting behaviour.

DRESS TO IMPRESS

First and foremost, dress appropriately for the meeting. You do not want how or what you dress to be a talking point or a distraction.

There is no set uniform, but as a rule of thumb if you want to be treated as an equal by a politician, dress like one. If you are a company representative but not a billionaire, I would advise against a T-shirt and jeans.

Both men and women should stick to a smart dress code, although ties can be tricky, as they are not always *de rigueur* for meetings in many countries. Nevertheless, you are aiming to dress similarly to the politician and so if in doubt it is best to wear one. If the politician turns out not to be wearing one, you have the opportunity (if you want to take it and sense it is right) to make an overt sign of reaching out by taking it off – or just do nothing and not make an issue of it at all. If the politician is wearing one and you are not, it is not a sensible option to produce one from your pocket and put it on.

Getting your dress right is important as it is a powerful tribal marker. Uniforms starkly mark out who is 'one of us' and who is a rival or enemy. Your dress choice sends out strong messages to the people you are meeting. It is reassuring if you look like them, and threatening or disturbing if you don't. At the same time, you need to be comfortable and not dress up if it really does not suit you or your organisation. You will be making a statement by being different and you have to be aware that you will conse-quently need to try a bit harder to gain acceptance and trust.

Once I turned up to a meeting all suited up, but the politi-cians working in an environment ministry all arrived in jeans and army surplus jackets. The difference in dress actually helped in the success of the meeting, as it was obvious from the outset that I had made an extra effort to find a rapport.

BEFORE THE MEETING
Before getting too close to the meeting room, take ten deep

breaths, inhaling through the nose and exhaling through your mouth.

This is not just about calming down and composing yourself. It is about releasing tension in the neck, shoulders and jaw, so making you look less rigid. It also helps to loosen your throat and voice box, thus preparing your voice for speaking in your natural tone.

To further prepare your voice, make 'bah – hah', or 'um – hum' sounds alternatively when exhaling. If this is going to sound too strange for your surroundings or entourage, go to the loo and do it there. This will mean that you won't start talking by clearing your throat or with a squeak.

This exercise is also good for preparing for telephone meetings, when you need to actively use the tone of your voice to be likeable. People can hear you smile, so make a conscious effort to smile when you talk on the telephone.

MAKE YOUR ENTRANCE

Walk in upright and not hunched up – keep your chin up and the rest will follow.

When you stand, keep your legs slightly spread to the width of your hips. It is a comfortable position and immediately makes you look grounded. You can project your voice easily and display confidence by comfortably taking up space without exaggerating.

Taking up space assertively is important not only when you enter but throughout the meeting. This gives you presence and the impression of confidence. This is the opposite of slinking in mouse-like, where your body signals are literally shrinking your space and presence.

If you stand with your feet together, you are unbalanced and unstable, so you look rigid and uncomfortable. To get the right position, put your feet together, splay your soles out and then straighten your feet by moving your heels – then relax and smile.

Look at the whole group, making fleeting eye contact with each participant. If there is an obvious leader, shake their hands firmly first. No hand wrestling here, just do not give a limp handshake.

The key point here is to make eye contact with everyone – it is inclusive to the whole group and non-aggressive. Remember, everyone in the room is important, and that includes the aides or personal assistants who greet you, offer you coffee and guide you to the room. They are usually very adept at assessing people and, if their bosses are sensible, they are asked for their opinion of you after the meeting.

You must also ensure that you smile. Smiles are catching. As the saying goes, 'Smile and the world smiles back at you.' It adds to your attractiveness and people will reciprocate, beginning the virtuous circle of getting them on side and open to listening to what you have to say.

However, there is one note of caution here – social cues can differ between cultures. Russians, for example, distrust people who smile too much; this can make it tricky for

Americans, who are usually great smilers. Take your cues from your audience if you are dealing with a culture you are not familiar with.

TAKING YOUR SEAT

Simple enough, you would have thought. But in reality, there is a minefield of social protocols.

Seats are indicators of power and hierarchy. 'Seat of government', 'throne', the 'hot seat' – all words illustrating that chairs are not simply just bits of furniture you happen to sit on. Happen to sit on the wrong one and you'll soon feel getting yourself out of it – this is at best an awkward moment.

When the seating is not clear, the situation can quickly descend into a game of musical chairs with everyone shuffling about but no one daring to actually sit down for fear of getting it wrong. Sensible organisers have a table plan sorted out in advance to avoid such social awkwardness and potential for dispute.

Politicians know seating is important. At summits and formal meetings, there are place names to avoid unnecessary friction. You will see the leaders' chairs exactly in line and at a side angle, firstly to show that both leaders are equal in status, but also to encourage negotiation. They are not opposite each other, which would illustrate division and opposition.

You have no choice about the seating arrangement. In a senior politician's office you usually have three options

– sitting across the desk from the politician, sitting around a meeting table or sitting informally on armchairs or sofas around a coffee table.

The choice rests with the politician, but, if asked, choose the armchairs. And if possible, sit alongside or at an angle to the politician rather than opposite. As with the summit, this puts you at equal status without being threatening. However, plonking yourself down on the politician's favoured chair is a no-no, so first ask where the politician usually sits. Even if the politician says there is no special chair, it is still better to leave them with the initiative and see where they are gravitating towards. Do not sit down before the politician.

If you are waiting and sitting already, get up and make it obvious that you are ready to move to another chair, even if you do end up sitting in exactly the same place. The body language has done its work and you have avoided upsetting the hierarchy of the tribe.

Office meeting tables are often round, making it easier to sit at an angle to the politician.

If you cannot avoid sitting opposite the politician, do not worry; use your body language to show you are open and engaging. The easiest way is to put your hands above the table, palm up when you start speaking. It immediately gives you an open and non-threatening stance which suggests you are willing to negotiate.

In a formal boardroom layout, you and your team will probably be sitting opposite the minister and their team. Right away, the signal goes out that you have different agendas, but you are at the same table, so it is still a place of negotiation.

When sitting down, the 'home' team usually chooses the side with the windows at their back. I was puzzled by how often this is the case, but then on seeing how thrones were often placed in front of windows in medieval courts, it struck me that it could only be about enhancing one's silhouette and thus the 'space' you are taking up – giving a heightened impression of size, presence and confidence. It is certainly not because your host thinks you will enjoy the view.

And you thought sitting down was simple.

DURING THE MEETING

Now you are all safely seated, look at everyone in the meeting and smile.

Before you speak, think about what you are going to say, breathe in and then speak when breathing out. I learnt this simple but effective technique from the Royal Academy of Dramatic Art acting school in London and it is invaluable.

Think, breathe, speak.

If you have looked around at everyone beforehand, you will naturally project your voice to all in the room. However, there should be a slight pause before you speak.

Pauses draw in the attention of your listeners and you can almost see them beginning to lean in to hear what you have to say. A pause cuts out distractions, focuses the attention on you and enhances the authority of your words and personality. A pause may be silent and invisible, but in fact it creates space for you and your words. A pause shows inner self-confidence. A pause gives you presence. Basically, a good pause is too good a tool not to have in your repertoire.

You may think I have gone over the top on the power of pausing. But think back to school – which teacher was more effective in silencing rowdy pupils? The one who shouted for silence, or the one who was obviously comfortable in their skin and just waited patiently and silently until everyone was quiet? I would put my money on the silent one.

Pausing stops you from rushing breathlessly into your point. Breathless and rushed points are not good for persuasive impact. You will come across as nervous and undermine the gravity of your point. Nervousness is catching and groups are unsettled by it.

Being nervous before making your point, or indeed before the meeting, is good – it gets the adrenaline going and sharpens your mind. However, it will make you tense. Tension will restrict your voice box and stiffen your neck, throat and shoulder muscles. This is why the breathing exercise is so important, as it allows you to balance out the nerves and to project confidence and authority. When you speak, the voice comes from the entire body. Slouching is a constraint, so sit upright and have your feet firmly and squarely on the ground. This makes you well-grounded and will calm you, making it easier to breathe and amplify your voice.

If you are not given an obvious chance to speak at the

beginning of the meeting, you should say something as soon as possible, even if it is trivial. This fixes you as a player around the table. The longer you leave it to speak, the harder is gets and the less people will regard your words when you do eventually speak. Not speaking soon marks you out as a follower, rather than a leader or someone of consequence, in the behavioural dynamics of the meeting space.

It is important to use your hands when you speak. Having your hands open and palms upwards makes what you are saying more attractive. Placing your hands palm downwards just above the table is a gesture of authority – use it when making your key points.

You must also listen actively – nod when important messages are made and smile. Lean forward slightly when the politician is making a point, or if you want to encourage them to continue speaking. This shows respect, keeping the hierarchical instincts happy and people at ease. Do not nod too often, though, as it signals that you are not really listening.

When you answer a question, resist the temptation to focus only on the person who asked it. Look around at everyone when you reply, or the discussion becomes a dialogue and therefore excludes them. Exclusion means they are less likely to focus on what you are saying and more easily distracted. If you are engaging them and they nod at your points, you are making an impact. However, you will have a tough job getting the people around the table to agree with your points if you have lost them by not looking their way.

If you want to know how the meeting is going, look at the position of your body in comparison to the politician's. If it is going well you will invariably be in the same position, as you will be subconsciously mimicking each other's movements. Mirroring makes people feel more comfortable. Whether leaning back to make a general point or leaning forward to make an important one, people are always on the move during a meeting if they are engaged. To show you are as well, move with them.

It pays to be aware of social cues given by the politician's body language. If your opposite moves forward in their chair, hands on knees as if to get up, this is a signal to wind up your point quickly. Missing it, or ignoring the movement, may be interpreted as rudeness.

In a similar vein, never have an open laptop in front of you – it shows a lack of respect and sends out signals that you are not part of the group. It renders your body language dumb – your eye contact is broken and distracted, so you miss body signals and cease to move in sync with the group. You can try to convince yourself that you are fully engaged in the meeting, but you have put up a barrier to your body. Close the laptop and keep it closed.

A distracted audience is hard to persuade – their minds are just not in the right space. Therefore, make sure you are not the distraction. One of the biggest sins you can commit is checking emails on your smartphone – this has all the down sides of looking at a laptop and multiplies the animosity of the group, due to your perceived disinterest in them and the discussion. It is one of the best ways to show disengagement from a group and to get their hackles up.

I have come across another great way to really ruin group engagement dynamics. At a senior-level panel debate, which was small and intimate (despite a slightly raised stage on which four politicians were seated in armchairs), we were amazed that one of them proceeded to leisurely do her make-up while the first politicians spoke. She put her vanity mirror away only when she was actually asked to speak and, on finishing, walked out of the room muttering that she had another engagement to go to. She was actually there to gather support for her cause, but no one bothered to listen to her.

As far as body language and group dynamics went, she did not go as far as peeing into the fireplace, but she might as well have done.

Other things to avoid during a meeting include: crossing your arms, biting your nails, vibrating your legs and slouching or hunching down. They signal that you are variously closed off to what the speaker is saying, offering little to the discussion, distracted and not interested in what the politician has to say. Whatever your feelings about the politician, don't allow your body language to let you down.

Lastly, when you are leading or playing a major role in a team, your people or pack are constantly monitoring your behaviour for emotional cues. If you look withdrawn, depressed or angry, the pack will instinctively pick up the feeling and mimic it. Careless body talk can cost you and your team success. You are literally setting the tone. If you are having a good day, great. If you are not, you must nevertheless pick yourself up, put a brave face on and play the part. Keep your posture relaxed, inclusive and open using hand gestures and eye contact. By making these signals, your pack is subconsciously picking up positive vibes. Do not let yourself go rigid and stare disconsolately at the table top.

I was once part of a small delegation meeting with an extreme right-wing parliamentarian. Worrying that I would disagree, possibly forthrightly, with the politician, I decided to remain discreet and silent in the background. At the end of the meeting I thought I had done a great job and avoided any unpleasant and unproductive arguments. Instead, my colleagues laughed, saying that they had never seen me so angry before in a political meeting. My body language had betrayed me – if they could see my anger, so could the politician. That was bad news for the outcome and a salutary reminder that body language always counts, even if you say nothing.

DEPARTURE

When it is time to leave, get up from your seat, lean across to shake hands and thank your host for their time and hospitality.

If you have been sitting round a large boardroom table, close down the psychological distance this has caused by promptly walking around and saying goodbye to each of your hosts. This leaves a good impression.

Gathering your papers together, shuffling off to the door only talking to your team, will not send out good signals, and nor will being seen to be in a rush to get out of the room. This leaves a sour note.

Do not think about how you feel the meeting went, as it will show in your face. Just focus on staying engaged right to the end.

All of these tips on body language are instinctive. They are the basis for polite and well-mannered behaviour, and avoiding the dangers of negative pack behaviour such as fights. However, being consciously aware of the power of body language and the instincts of pack and animal behaviour gives you a significant edge.

Politics is all about people and people appreciate good body language – so speak it well and don't pee in the proverbial fireplace.

THE ART OF PERSUASION

WHAT DO YOU FIND PERSUASIVE?

Persuasion is an art form and you need to work to get better at it. When faced by politicians, you have a limited amount of time to be persuasive. Think about whom you really find persuasive, for example a news anchor, a priest, a teacher, a doctor or a car salesman. What was it about them that made them so persuasive? Was it their oratory, their gravitas, the way they make you feel special or their humbleness?

What makes these figures persuasive is that they create a sense of safety. They are seen as trustworthy authority figures and they are good at striking up a rapport and making you feel that you matter. You might question the inclusion of the car salesman, but if he is good, he is successfully selling people their most expensive purchase after their house. (I have also included the salesman as businesspeople have similar reputation issues in the world of politics.)

What it boils down to is that to persuade anyone in a political meeting you need to be credible. Without credibility, you may as well stay at home.

The style you use comes down to your personality, so use the one you are most comfortable with and think will work best in the circumstances. There are four typical styles:

- An assertive style – where you are stating what you need by setting out your expectations clearly, speaking with authority and not being shy about interrupting.
- A bridging style – where you show you are listening by acknowledging the points made by others, asking questions to explore others' views, reflecting and summarising what the audience are thinking.
- An attractive style – where you are looking to build optimism and trust. A 'yes we can!' style that lends itself

to a story-like structure of setting a scene, describing an event and what it means for the audience. Priests use this when building on the lessons of parables to influence a congregation.

- A persuasive style – where you are explaining by making a proposal, backing it up with the two or three good reasons, stating the opposing view and then re-stating your proposal.

CREDIBILITY AND TRUSTWORTHINESS

Your strongest card is that you are the expert in your own business or technology. Build on this to transform yourself into the authority figure, emanating gravitas and trustworthiness. When you talk, your audience will know that what you say matters. What matters to politicians and officials is that you have the solution to their problem.

BE ATTRACTIVE AND ENGAGING

People are more likely to be persuaded by people they find attractive. Your message will be more attractive and engaging when delivered dramatically, by which I mean using loaded words and images.

In a fight over waste incineration in July 2018, an activist group had to sell the problem that 226 tonnes of particulates (PM10 and PM2.5) are emitted from incinerators each year in the UK (the activists' figures). This is a dry, jargon-filled and uninspiring message. How do you gauge or imagine 226 tonnes of particulates? Is it a lot? Who knows what PM10 and PM2.5s are? Further, 'emitted' is hardly a word to get excited about. However, if you put it in terms such as 'Incinerator pollution is the equivalent of a quarter of a million lorries each travelling 75,000 miles' as the activists did, you have conjured up an image and combined it with the threatening word 'pollution'. You will get political attention.

If you look at the dry, over-long and complex paper that has been put together by an assortment of association and company people and approved by corporate lawyers, you may despair at trying to sell it to a politician.

First off, prepare a quarter-page short summary in plain language to get a focused, jargon-free message in simple but intriguing terms that you can use to sell the key points of your argument. If this is not an option, put the paper to one side, just think of the three key points you want to make and say them as it comes naturally during the meeting. Never look at or read out from the paper – your delivery is guaranteed to be dull as ditch water if you do, and dull is unattractive.

Attractive does not mean having film star looks. What it means is being engaging – being totally interested in what people are telling you. How often is it heard that the great persuaders are past masters of this? Looks are irrelevant to being engaging with people; making them think that they matter makes them more predisposed to agreeing with you, and this is what is important.

DELIVERING THE SOLUTION

You may think that the draft policy or anticipated political decision that you are discussing is wrongheaded – quite likely, in fact, as you are out there meeting politicians to try to influence it. But you need to avoid getting into an argument and definitely avoid saying that the politicians are wrong. If you really want to divert the ponderous super tanker that is the ship of state, you need to imitate the action of the tugboat and nudge the ship in your direction. Trying to stop it in its tracks usually means that you get run over.

The best nudge you have is to present a solution to the politician's problem, and the way to introduce it is to say that you are looking for a solution and have some ideas. People are most influenced by what they hear first and opening up with 'let us find a solution' is a friendly, constructive and intriguing way to begin.

When couching your message, say that you have been talking to other 'players' and putting your case to them with interesting results. People are naturally more persuaded by messages that don't appear to be aimed specifically at them. If you have a presentation (e.g. papers, slides and brochures), say that they have been prepared for officials, MPs or other stakeholders, not specifically for your target at the meeting.

Do not be afraid to amplify the threat, as long as you do not overdo it and drift into the realm of hyperbole. You have to remain believable and authoritative, but making the threat loom larger gives you room to present a 'smaller' solution.

This is a type of technique known as 'anchoring': if you lead with the 'big' problem, the 'small' solution sounds a great deal. Using the example of the car salesman, if you tell him that you need a good car for driving around town, he will reply that the ideal car could cost you up to £50,000, but luckily he has a great one available at £35,000, just for you. He has anchored your expectations to the £50,000 figure and made £35,000 sound like you're getting a great deal, even if you were determined to only spend £30,000 when you walked into the showroom.

GETTING THE MOOD MUSIC RIGHT

You will know the discussion is really going your way when the politician adopts your idea as their own. Encourage this and let them feel that the idea is theirs.

So how do you get there? The most important thing is to ensure you are not doing all of the talking. Probably the biggest mistake to make at a political meeting is that, having worked so hard on what you are going to say, it all comes out in a big, long rush, and you have basically talked out the opportunity to get a discussion going. Equally, if you are conscious about trying to avoid doing this, you may promise yourself that you will kick off with a question. However, if the question lasts for more than forty seconds, it is too long and you are talking out discussion time again. Instead, prepare a couple of twenty-second questions in advance.

If the first questions can be readily answered with a yes,

you are already starting to nudge the politician into a positive mind-set where saying yes is comfortable.

NUDGING

You should start out by saying – rhetorically or otherwise – 'I think we can all agree that it is important that we move forward to finding a solution.' This should at least get you a friendly nod.

If it does, you will have achieved three important things: you have made a positive start by securing a 'yes'; by using 'we', you have given the impression that this is a joint effort to find a solution; and, subliminally, you have positioned the politician into making a commitment to finding a solution. This is your first nudge.

People want to be consistent. By getting a 'yes', you are already making it psychologically difficult for the politician to go backwards and say that it is a bad idea to find a solution and a bad idea to talk with you about it.

You also need to let the politician do a great deal of talking. While this is happening, you have to do your best to see things from their point of view, be sympathetic to their ideas and nod along. When asking your questions, ask for their views and principles on the issue at hand. Then be quick-witted and align your points with them. Phrases such as 'I totally agree with your point that such and such has to be dealt with,' and 'Building on your excellent idea...' are useful phrases to have in your lexicon, as you are essentially mimicking or mirroring the politician, making them more comfortable and more committed to the idea. This is your second nudge.

Now you need to keep the momentum going. Use social proof (i.e. saying that 'the majority of people/leading academics/a broad range of parliamentarians/a majority of countries in Europe would agree with you') is a powerful way to nudge. You are making the course of action feel more secure, as others also want to follow it.

People want to feel safe and make the safe choice. Advertisers tap into this psychological need to feel safe and follow social norms all the time. You want the best for your pet, so it is a safe choice to buy one that nine out of ten pet owners choose – and it is the same with political decisions.

Another tactic you can use is to appeal to their nobler motives. You should know their background and use this knowledge to say that the course of action you are discussing is good for democracy, free trade and the economy, the environment or tackling crime, for example. You can also appeal to their political ambitions and self-esteem by saying that it will be popular, win votes and send out a clear and powerful political signal.

These appeals create a need. People want self-esteem, safety and admiration. Our social needs – to be popular, prestigious or similar to others – are deep-seated and powerful levers you can use to get to your ideal situation – in which the politician absorbs your arguments, adopts them and starts to act on them.

If you are going great guns and the politician looks as though they are being persuaded, turn the conversation towards how the solution can tackle the real or perceived difficulties. Difficulties act as a dampener to ambition and enthusiasm, so it is time to say that you'll be working hard in supporting the politician and that you need their help.

PUT WORDS INTO ACTIONS

How can you help the politician and how can they help you? And, more importantly, how can you ensure they will actually take action?

The situation will dictate what the help could be. It could be raising your issue by writing a letter to a newspaper, speaking at a conference, holding a press conference or putting forward an amendment to draft laws. Having a request ready is part of your preparation.

There are a few tactics that you can employ to persuade the politician to act.

One is to ask for a small action first, and then ask for something bigger. Just like with nudging, if the politician says yes to the first request, you are in a favourable position to getting a positive response to the second one. Why say no, when they have already said yes? The small request could be asking if they would be prepared to send a letter to the editor of the *Financial Times* and suggesting that you would be happy to draft one if needed. If they say yes, you can ask if they would be happy to follow it up with a press conference. As they have technically agreed to help you by agreeing to act, it is a behavioural logic that they will follow and agree to the press conference.

However, this may also work the other way round. Start with a big ask that will probably be turned down and then put forward a smaller appeal. People feel obliged to say yes after refusing an initial request. Using our example, you could ask the politician if they would travel to another country to address a conference. On refusal, you may instead suggest that they could hold a press conference near their office instead.

A supporting tactic is to give a gift just before making your request. This should not be anything of real value – we are definitely not talking about bribes here. It can be anything from a brochure to a paperweight with your corporate logo on it. It will probably go into the bin after the meeting, but it has a psychological effect – the act of giving a gift tends to make people want to reciprocate in turn.

Another effective ploy is to use the appeal of scarcity. If you suggest that you are planning to do only one press conference, you have turned it into a unique opportunity for the politician.

Finally, if you have to talk about figures and funding, use the anchoring technique. For example: 'Experts have told us that we could solve this problem with €10 million; I am sure that we could actually deliver the essentials with €8 million, but we would have to act fast.' Here, you have bolstered your case by citing authoritative experts, made €8 million sound a good deal and added to its attraction by making it an exclusive opportunity.

IF IT ALL GOES WRONG

It all seems easy when the meeting is going from strength to strength – but what do you do if it takes a turn for the worse?

Things can go wrong straight away. I was once waiting for a German minister in his office to talk about aircraft noise. He then came through the door shouting that he did not see why he was meeting us, that he disagreed with all our points, and that we and his entourage were wasting his time – all at full volume and in good, correct but very bad-tempered English.

We took a deep breath, said nothing and smiled.

When the tirade blew itself out, we offered to pour him a coffee, which seemed to mollify him a bit. He was also pleased when we said that we totally sympathised with him and his voters, as no one likes noisy aircraft flying over their homes. This was a good tactic to use, as he loved talking about his electorate and it gave us an opening to shift the discussion on to the latest technological advances in quieter aircraft and how he could help. Within minutes, the heat had gone and we actually ended up having a good meeting with him.

The order of play was to show empathy, appeal to his values

and ask for his help. It is important to phrase the question correctly: 'What if?' helps remove ego from the discussion (i.e. 'What if there were quieter aircraft?'); 'We need your help' engages the politician; and 'Would it be helpful?' shifts the focus from the problem to the solution.

This was a most explosive start to a meeting, but it comes with the territory. Politicians, especially if they have an audience, sometimes choose to attack you to show that they will not be influenced by corporations. It is a popular move, but no less uncomfortable if you are the one under fire.

Apparently using someone's first name triggers a pleasure response in their brain chemistry. If the meeting is going well, use it. If the meeting is going badly, definitely use it. You have very little time to get the meeting back on an even keel, so use anything that helps.

Do not get into a shouting match. Do not cross your arms and harrumph. Just draw that breath, keep silent, smile and focus on engaging your opponent. Talleyrand, Napoleon's aristocratic Foreign Minister, said that pausing to take a pinch of snuff before answering a difficult question was the secret to his diplomatic skill. He knew what he was talking about, as he not only worked for Napoleon, but the King afterwards – and he avoided the guillotine.

EMPATHY

Of all the skills and tactics you need to bring to bear when meeting politicians, probably the most important quality you need is empathy. Without it, you will be at a loss as to where the other party is coming from; without it, you will have difficulty striking up a rapport in a good meeting, let alone in one where everything starts to go wrong; and without it, you will have problems correctly analysing your progress in the political battle.

To some it comes naturally – others have to work at it. And some who lack it are sensible enough to have empathetic people with them to explain what is actually going on.

THE AFTERMATH

Once the meeting is over, you need to ask: did you achieve anything? If you got the minister to agree to your press conference, bravo – this is something solid. Otherwise, you need to reflect on how you felt it went. Gut reaction is a good indicator, as your senses pick up more subconsciously than you may realise.

You also learn a lot about what the other person is thinking, planning and concerned about from their questions. Always note them down and review them afterwards – this will develop your insights into what is really making them tick.

As you may guess from this chapter, you can never over-emphasise the importance of performing well in meetings. Bad meetings – when you say too little, or say too much, or what you do say is unmemorable – will, at best, fail to move your campaign forward and, at worst, damage your reputation. Go into meetings with a well-prepared, simple and persuasive message, and a clear aim. Finally, in the meeting itself, be forever conscious that it is your body language that is doing most of the communicating – this is your key to being attractive, authoritative and persuasive, and will give you the confidence and presence to carry your points.

PULLING POLITICAL LEVERS

When you are meeting and persuading politicians across Europe, having a basic idea about the kind of politician you will meet is important so that you can adapt your message delivery.

It used to be simple: politicians were socialist, conservative or liberal – the establishment parties and political families. Now there are new kids on the block holding influential positions that need to be dealt with – environmentalists (not so new), nationalists and ideologues. This section starts with a basic primer on the trends in European politics and then moves on to take a closer look at a national level.

The emphasis here is on dealing with governments, as they are the centres of power in the European political set-up.

EUROPEAN POLITICAL FAMILIES – NEW FACES AND NEW TENSIONS

Post-war twentieth-century European politics were stable as far as political parties were concerned. In each country there was a party or grouping on the left and one on the right (I say 'groupings', as countries like Belgium and the Netherlands love their small parties and coalition governments) and there was generally a bipartisan and positive attitude in foreign affairs towards NATO and, later, the European institutions.

There were very few new parties or ideologies of note to emerge. Trade unions and business confederations were sometimes so closely aligned with the political structure they became part of the political institutions. There was also little movement of people across frontiers.

The big aim in the West was rebuilding after the Second World War with steady progress towards building in-depth alliances and coalescing economies in Europe. On the economic front, there was a spurt forward on economic integration, with the push from the 1980s onwards for the creation of a single market.

Then in 1989 the Berlin Wall came down.

With Russia retreating from its political hegemony in central Europe, this was a moment of great hope for the future and prompted celebrations that the Cold War had finally ended. The European Economic Community evolved into a more tightly knit European Union and pushed ahead with a rapid expansion into the old Soviet Bloc central European countries and launched the euro. All was apparently rosy in the European garden.

But it did not last long. Political systems that were designed for the Cold War became dated. Environmentalist 'green' parties emerged and became a real force in European politics, particularly in the north. Nationalism and populism, which were discredited after the Second World War and held at bay during the Cold War, re-emerged as political forces as electorates tired of the grip that their traditional political classes held on the political system.

Populist, non-establishment extremist parties attracted growing popular support across 'old' Europe (i.e. Finland, Denmark, Belgium, the Netherlands, France, the UK, Italy, Spain and even Sweden).

This trend of disenchantment with the political establishment seemed to be on fast forward in 'new' Europe, with the election of populists and nationalists in Poland, the Czech Republic and Hungary, and even seemingly stable countries like Slovenia.

Probably the biggest and most surprising victory more recently for the anti-establishment was Emmanuel Macron in France. He created a new party, was elected as President and secured a majority in the legislature, all the while offering hope and optimism, and support for the EU.

However, probably the biggest casualty has been the UK. Through a combination of a complacent establishment and populist fears about immigration, it has put itself on a course veering away from its European allies and economic partners by voting to leave the EU.

Whether these populists in Europe are a long-lasting phenomenon or a flash in the pan, as a business leader you still need to deal with them. Many will have their hands on the levers of power, joining the establishment parties as those you need to talk to.

The most profound impact of the new parties has been in central Europe. In countries with immature institutional systems like Poland and Hungary, not only have the parliamentarians and ministers changed, but their civil services have been cut back drastically and politically cleansed in large-scale lustration exercises, even down to the low-level officials and agency leaders. This has broken the continuity, expertise and stability of their administrations. Many incomers are bright and energetic, but it will still take a while until their administrations regain their stability and expertise.

Turning to the establishment parties – there are the left socialist-leaning politicians, the right conservative-leaning politicians, the liberal in-between politicians and the new-establishment green politicians. These are just the labels that situate them on the political spectrum and are only really helpful in the context of their specific country, given the huge variation of polities across Europe. A socialist, pro-market

UK Prime Minister like Tony Blair is a very different animal from a statist Swedish socialist.

Putting these political variations aside, when lobbying few European politicians will be impressed by how much profit you are making, or your share price performance. What they want to know is how many people you employ and your future intentions regarding investment and job creation in their country. After that, the conservatives and liberals are likely to be more interested in market forces and productivity levels, while the socialists and greens are more likely to be distrustful of market forces and ask where the state can take action.

The populist and nationalist politician will also be interested in jobs, but much more eager to seek radical non-establishment solutions that play well to a populist mind-set, but lack economic sense.

Dealing with dogmatists and ideologues – the true socialist, the dyed-in-the-wool nationalist or the green-eyed environmentalist – is difficult if you are a business pragmatist wanting to talk rationally about economics and the need for political certainty, but it still needs to be done. You need to avoid getting into no-win ideological battles and work hard to identify common ground, and get your points across and noted down.

Overall, the old way of anticipating a meeting with a conservative or a socialist, and sometimes a liberal, has radically altered. Now you have to be ready to meet and to present your case to politicians with a wider range of political views.

FINDING YOUR WAY AROUND EUROPE

If you have a political problem with a European angle, you will need to talk to other governments than your own. It is not a great surprise that generally people and companies are comfortable in lobbying their own governments, but can be reluctant to lobby others. This is a mistake, as national governments in Europe wield the most power in the European system. If you are looking to find the most powerful political leverage points you need to be prepared to meet with them. Once, when working on a European policy, I had to talk to over twenty governments to get the political leverage I needed in order to win.

Politicians – from officials up to ministers – vary considerably between countries, although they are essentially doing the same job. The variables are driven by history and culture. When you lobby politicians in another country, you should familiarise yourself with the basics of the country's history, as well as its political priorities, structure and attitudes. This will make the meetings go much more smoothly and give you a better chance to succeed.

In some meetings, you may be welcomed warmly, but more often you will get a cautious welcome that may feel a bit frosty at first. This is because lobbying governments in Europe is not the norm, unlike in America where it is seen as part of the law-making process. However, if you are polite, make fair and clear points and bring good information, the meeting soon warms up.

Language can be a barrier. You are lucky if you speak English, as it has become the lingua franca for politicians dealing with European matters. Otherwise, use an interpreter.

This section is designed to encourage and prepare you to engage with foreign governments when you need to. It covers the main political blocs and will give you a flavour of the different types of decision maker you will find in Europe.

GERMANY

The first thing you need to get your head around, especially if you come from a country with centralised systems like France, is how regionalised Germany is. Stemming from its post-war constitution, a lot of the real power resides with the states, known as the *Länder*, and not in Berlin. If you want to talk about details of energy policy, noise at airports or government aid for technological development, you need to talk to the *Länder*.

The civil service is political above a certain level, in the sense that the civil servant's political party and thus patronage are known. You have to take this into account when facing a senior state secretary, for example, as they will have more influence if their political masters are from the same party.

The different ministries are very protective of their turf and spend a lot of energy fighting each other. This can be helpful, but not if you have one ministry forming a policy that might be nixed by a competing ministry just when you think the plan is finalised. As in most political systems, the powerful ministries are finance, foreign affairs, trade and industry, but the environment ministry also holds a lot of sway in Germany, especially when the ruling coalition includes the Green Party.

Germany is the largest economy and trader in Europe with significant foreign investment, but this does not mean that its political system is open. It is extremely cliquey – if you are in the club there is a whole system of political groups and official fora in which to interact with officials and ministers. Politicians will meet outsiders but are reluctant to do so during the internal debating and formulation phase.

Ministries are well-resourced and well-equipped to study issues in depth, and they also have close contacts with technical organisations, like Max Planck Institutes, and with consultancies that are often spin-offs from universities.

Getting on the inside is tricky, as you need to be part of the club – even when you think you are, you're not. In the 1990s, when climate change became a big issue, German carmakers purposely held a meeting in August (when the factories were closed and the executives on holiday, meaning that not all the carmakers were around the table) to decide on their policy, therefore excluding Ford and GM (Opel), despite them being long-established car producers in Germany.

As a side note, Germans can be shy about lobbying, so they may be talking quite intensely with their government, although they are loath to admit it. This can make working with them in alliances trickier than it should be.

Even so, allying with Germans, if you manage it, is great for a campaign. The officials are thorough and they are reliable attendees at European meetings. When they do speak, they carry weight in the room – many smaller countries, especially central Europeans, will take their lead from Germany.

AUSTRIA

Austria is another clubby outfit. Ministries only really like to work with well-established associations that act more like quasi-government organs. Put another way, politicians see associations as an arm of government and do not appreciate hearing openly dissenting views from them. If you are an outsider and you have an opposing view, you may want to see if other Austrian companies agree with you and establish a new association.

Officials are often surprised if you want to see them, as they have their official channels to deal with the associations, but they usually agree. If you do meet with them, it helps enormously if you have an Austrian with you. It is also a good idea to aim closer to the minister, as their advisors are usually younger and more open to outside argumentation than the tradition-bound lower levels.

DENMARK

Danes are ever-reliable attendees at international meetings and nearly always vocal. They are very active in environmental policy, often taking extreme positions in this area. They are tenacious when plugging their case and are influential in European discussions.

Their priority is always Denmark, to the extent that if they do not get their way, they will press ahead with making Danish laws, even if they know they are likely to be attacked by other European countries. For example, Denmark famously went ahead with banning lead in products despite the fact that it would be struck down under EU single market law, as the ban would have prevented imports from its European partners from being sold in Denmark. In the end it was persuaded to back down and abandon its legislation, but not before it had got an undertaking that the EU would itself introduce lead-free laws. This was great political arm-twisting from a small country.

Danes are simultaneously Eurosceptic and best in class at enacting European single market laws. It sounds contradictory, but it means that while they are independent minded and prefer clear legal frameworks, they are also determined to make the most of the new markets that single market legislation opened up for them.

The Danish civil service is pretty efficient and well-funded. Officials have solid links with agencies and technical institutes, but often distrust corporate interests, even Danish ones. At the same time, their organisation and decision-making are transparent and they will accept meetings with industry if you are persistent. Nevertheless, you do need to focus on building up trust. They are quite happy to make a policy relying only on their own research and technical institutes without input from industry.

I have mentioned Denmark's love for the environment. Indeed, an environmental party is not needed in their Parliament, as they are all green!

All in all, the Danes punch above their weight on the European scene and if you can get them on side, you will benefit. However, if you oppose them, you will discover their obstinate determination to get their way.

ITALY

Jumping to the other end of Europe, dealing with the south is a completely different kettle of fish from the north. Italy is normally a Europhile and a serial offender when it comes to enacting European legislation.

Like Germany, it is highly regionalised and it can be difficult to find the real levers of power. Mayors and regional powers are influential, but can be bypassed by Rome (when it suits Rome). Italian officials can be highly distrustful of non-Italian corporate arguments while their links with Italian industries can be weak.

A lot depends on the personalities of the department heads and the officials. I know this may sound like a stereotype, but the Italian system is chaotic and there is no standard way of doing things. A typical meeting with government is pretty formal and ad hoc debate is unusual. You will probably meet a minister or senior official flanked by junior officials, many of them women. You can rely on the latter being well-informed and conscientious, but you cannot rely on senior participants taking the time to be well-briefed. It can be a frustrating business if you are not prepared for this.

The attendance of Italian officials at international meetings is erratic. If there is an issue of importance to Italy, you won't see any Italian officials in the committee rooms during build-up discussions, but suddenly a minister will arrive and create merry hell at a ministerial meeting.

This no-show and last-minute rage approach to negotiations does not usually work well. However, a notable example when it did was when the EU was deciding where to locate its food agency. In the build-up negotiations, Finland emerged as the likely candidate, but at a European summit, the boisterous Italian Prime Minister Silvio Berlusconi demanded that it should be based in Italy. He won, but it would have been more efficient, diplomatically speaking, for Italy to have done the build-up work without the last-minute histrionics.

Internationally, Italy punches below its weight politically and is an uncertain ally. Within the country, due to its regionalism, it is best starting to work with your regions and establish a good base before looking to go higher. The system is complex and you would be well-advised to work with Italians to get things done. Lobbying is not often done by industry groups in Italy, and you need patience and persistence to get them to be active on your behalf.

What the Italians do have is a flexible attitude to finding solutions. Italy is a major partner in the development of the newest US fighter aeroplane. Finding the money to pay for this with a population not very keen on military spending was a political poser. The solution was to bury the funding of the fighter purchase in the research budget of the industry ministry. Only in Italy...

SPAIN

Spain is highly regionalised and is, in some ways, still a maturing polity prone to instability. Since joining the EU, its main interests were securing EU funds and protecting its agriculture and fisheries, while trying to re-energise its industry. It has become a lot richer and has moved on from acting the poor cousin.

Officials who used to be no-shows are now attending international meetings and have started to be more vocal. Political instability, public sector cutbacks and debt crises have held it back, but I think that it is well-placed to become more influential internationally. Given its need to attract international investment, it has a more pro-trade and pro-inward investment attitude than countries like France.

Similar to Italy, higher-level meetings can be formal and

stilted. Initial meetings with officials can also be difficult, but things do warm up after the first couple of times. You have to realise that trust cannot be established in one meeting alone. Structures for liaising with industry associations are often weak, but I found that after the initial stickiness, officials and politicians welcome the input and topic expertise that even non-Spanish industry can bring.

PORTUGAL

It must be irritating for the Portuguese to be forever linked with Spain and it is a big mistake to treat the two nationalities and political systems the same way.

Portugal has suffered economically and its public sector has been downsized. It has a centralised political system. It wants to attract investment and, unlike the larger European economies, it does not have 'national champions' (i.e. very large companies whose economic interests are seen as indivisible from those of the nation) making life difficult for you politically, in stark contrast to a country like Germany, where national champions have the political clout to exclude non-German interests.

Meetings, even at a high level, feature debate and argument. They have a frank manner that can catch you off guard at first, but it makes them a lot easier to analyse and assess. If they can do something for you, they will say so. If they cannot, they will say so.

Portugal may be small, but as its economy gets back on its feet I expect it to be more active internationally and a worthwhile ally to have.

IRELAND

Ireland is another small, politically centralised country, but one which definitely punches above its weight in the political arena. With a large diaspora in the US, it nearly always has support from the other side of the Atlantic and has attracted a lot of US investment.

Since it joined the EU, it has grown rapidly from worrying only about agriculture and securing EU funding for its infrastructure, to successfully attracting international investment and boasting a growing manufacturing sector.

Ireland is blessed with a good education system, good communication skills and a love for politics and political debate. Like Denmark, the Irish political system is close-knit and village-like. What it does better at, though, is having an informal network of Irish diaspora that transcends political parties. The 'Irish mafia' is an influential force in Brussels and makes them good allies to have.

Meetings with Irish politicians are relatively easy to set up and they are generally interested in what you have to say and like to discuss things through. The networks and ways of getting things done in Irish politics are characteristically informal.

FINLAND

Finland is a large country geographically, but has a small population. Highly independent, it has spent most of its history fighting off its neighbours – a difficult one being Russia, but the Finns managed it. This makes them quietly determined and somewhat fatalistic.

They are wary of lobbying, as they do not want to be seen as being biased or influenced by certain companies. In some ways, it is an advantage being an outsider as there is no suspicion of favouritism. As an outsider, it is quite easy to find out whom to speak to and secure a meeting. However, you must be patient in your dealings, as Finns are slow to commit and will not say yes until ready to do so. But once committed, they act.

They are good attendees at European meetings, but are rarely very vocal. I have always found them to be highly pragmatic and less idealistic than their neighbours in Sweden.

SWEDEN

In contrast, Sweden is formal in attitude and favours formal ways of going about things. Swedes are seemingly open and flexible, but in reality are clubby and stubborn.

Politics in Sweden is a quieter affair than in Denmark and usually less Eurosceptic. Swedes take their laws seriously and are good attendees at international meetings and negotiations. Swedish politicians and officials are often idealist in working to protect the people; this can make them less than pragmatic. They may concede that there are other ways of doing things, but will follow up by saying, 'In Sweden, we do it differently.'

In one case, a French company was importing fully certified and tested equipment, but the products were nevertheless deemed unsafe as they did not comply with Swedish standards. The importer was threatened with a ban. The best advice the importer got was to knuckle down and do it the Swedish way. Blandishments to the ministry saying that the ban broke EU law did not succeed.

Sweden is an important player in the Nordic Council, where parliamentarian cooperation between Sweden, Denmark, Finland, Iceland and Norway has led to the emergence of a united bloc which promotes issues like climate change and cleaning up the Baltic Sea.

The environment is an important issue in Sweden. The relevant ministries and agencies are well-funded, active and have close contacts with Swedish academic and technical institutes.

Decision-making in Sweden, within nearly all types of group and institution, is surprisingly inclusive and involves much internal debate. This can make things a bit slow, but they are methodical and follow processes that they are loath to short-circuit.

Sweden has a diversified workforce. Whether you are meeting ministers and senior advisors or working officials, they are likely to be women, in stark contrast to countries like Greece.

Getting to meet with politicians is relatively easy. At the meetings, they give clear explanations of their decision-making processes and patiently hear out your arguments. However, securing actual action is tricky. Swedes avoid direct confrontation and if they disagree with you, they will nod politely, but do nothing. If pressed to explain why no action was taken, they will courteously say that the matter was discussed internally and a collective decision was made not to act. This can be trying if you are not used to it.

Swedish companies have good links to their associations and interest groups and have solid links with their government. This makes them highly influential decision makers and good allies, as they know how the Swedish system works. The companies do not like to admit to having such influence and the government is equally shy about it, but it is there.

In the close-knit community of Sweden there is a high level of confidence that the political class will act responsibly with the large amounts of tax they take from the population. Any corruption, even relatively minor, is frowned upon as it breaks this social contract, and the politicians implicated are quickly removed.

BELGIUM

Things are rather different in Belgium – there is little confidence that politicians will be careful and deal cleanly with taxpayers' money. Corruption scandals regularly erupt but are met with a shrug of the shoulders by the populace at large, and the political class, seemingly inured to it, just carry on.

The low level of confidence in politicians has resulted in a highly fragmented and regionalised political system.

This fragmentation of power can be exasperating to deal with. Once, a pressure group wanted to use a horse outside the European Parliament building to promote its cause. Unfortunately for them, the road marked the border between two borough councils. It ended up that the horse got permission to walk on one half of the road, but not the other. As the group could not guarantee that the horse would not meander, the plan had to be abandoned.

Regionalisation in Belgium is taken seriously. Split into four regions, each has its own Parliament, ministers and ministries, and there are reputedly over 1,000 ministers in Belgium.

Trying to find the correct levers of power within this system can be fiendishly complicated. There is a lack of oversight between the officials attending international meetings and their ministers. You think Belgian officials are stating the official Belgian government view at an international meeting, only for the minister to say separately that it was not. You walk out of the minister's office still not knowing who is really making the decisions.

A lot of patience is called for in dealing with a system seemingly designed to be inefficient. It should certainly give you a clue as to why the Belgians have a reputation for being masters of finding a compromise.

THE NETHERLANDS

The Netherlands is a small, rich and densely populated country that is seen from the outside as a tightly knit, well-governed and centralised state. While the government is indeed centralised, 'tightly knit' is not such a good description of the country's inhabitants. There are sharp social differences between a Protestant north and a Catholic south, and between the liberal urbanites of Amsterdam and Rotterdam and the rest of the country. Its politics has, however, resolved into a relatively harmonious system balancing the different social and religious groups.

If the Dutch have a lot of confidence that their politicians will be careful with their tax euros, they have little faith that the European Union will. It is annoying for them that, while they do not have a lot of voting power in the EU due to their small size, they pay a lot into EU coffers due to their wealth.

The Netherlands has an excellent record in implementing EU legislation as it can clearly see the commercial advantage of the single market, but the money issue means that the Dutch are strong supporters of deregulation and strongly sceptical about seeing their money funnelled to less economically secure nations. Hence, the rise of the extreme right in a country more associated with liberal attitudes.

As successful traders, the Dutch are keen to push the free

trade and single market agendas, and are usually found supporting the UK position.

The Dutch civil service is efficient and well-resourced. They have regular contacts with 'their' industries, although the debate between the two sides can be robust. Approaching from the outside, it is not difficult to gain an audience as they are quite open to talking about the political debate. This is in contrast with the Poles and the Germans, who dislike talking openly about the politics of decision-making.

Dutch civil servants are regular attendees at European and international meetings, and are vocal when necessary. They are good at chairing EU meetings and finding compromises. This is a different attitude to many bigger countries that are happy to hold tenaciously to their national position, even if this delays getting an EU agreement.

Similar to Germany and the Nordics, environmental issues are important to the Dutch, but they are generally more pragmatic and consider the cost benefits of legislation seriously.

LITHUANIA

Lithuanian politicians are similar to the Nordics in their forthrightness, but they are less formal. Ministers are young, the officials younger and most of them are women. They always start meetings on time.

If Nordic countries worry about the environment, the Baltics worry about their neighbour Russia. Russia can seem a distant threat when you're sitting in Dublin, but in Vilnius you quickly learn that Russia supplies its energy, and the minister you are meeting with could well have been imprisoned by them. Lithuania has suffered for its independence from the Russian Empire, but there is a strong urge to move on and modernise itself. It joined the euro as it was strongly symbolic of its move away from Russia and its embedding in the EU.

Lithuania, like its Baltic state neighbours Latvia and Estonia, is keen on inward investment, supporting free trade and, like Ireland, its politicians are happy to meet outsiders.

POLAND

To say the very least, Poland has had a troubled history with its neighbours Germany and Russia. The first things you notice when staying in Warsaw are the photographs in hotels and restaurants of what it looked like before it was flattened in the Second World War. History, and a sombre one at that, is all around you. Joining the EU has given Poland the chance to regain its pre-eminence as an independent power and it has thrived economically.

Even so, there is a Eurosceptic streak in its politics and Polish politicians can be feisty with their European counterparts. They have burnt diplomatic bridges and this has prevented them from being the major power broker in central Europe given its size and economy.

As for lobbying in Warsaw, this is an interesting experience. There are high levels of distrust towards corporate interests that can make initial contact frosty. The links between politics and industry associations, which are such useful political levers in other countries, are nascent at best in Poland. This is a common trait with the other former communist states. Officials are often ignorant about industry realities, but once the initial suspicions are overcome, officials appreciate the knowledge you can share with them.

Polish political institutions like ministries and agencies are not as mature as those in countries such as Germany, France and the UK. They lack solid roots to remain stable and withstand changes in the political winds. The latest government has done a thorough job of getting rid of officials in the ministries and agencies that it sees as politically tainted from the previous regime. This makes it difficult to engage with the government due to such a big turnover of personnel and the loss of expertise.

HUNGARY

The Hungarians are similar to the Poles in that they have a proud history and are quite feisty about their independence, whether from the Habsburg Empire or the Soviet one. Similarly to Poland, the ruling party is very nationalistic and does not like to be pushed around by Brussels.

They have also cut back on and purged a lot of their officials. There used to be a stable system, where you got to know the officials who were dealing with your issue. However, the personnel changes have made contacts harder to maintain.

Links between government and industry in Hungary can be weak. I once asked an official if they had requested input from industry. 'Of course,' he replied, adding, 'I emailed the industry association we thought was the right one, but we got no reply.'

Hungary has deterred investment with some of its erratic behaviour, for example by imposing extraordinary taxes aimed specifically at international investors in its telecoms, banking and retail setors. Once, during a meeting between major corporations and a previous President, the group was told by the President that, as investors had profited from the past growth of Hungary, they now had the opportunity to repay the Hungarian state. He concluded on a light note, saying that Hungary was now even more open to new investments.

Such attitudes make engagement with Hungarian politicians tricky to say the least.

FRANCE

France is probably the most centralised country in Europe and its President is easily the most powerful head of state. In most other countries, heads of state are ceremonial; in France, the President is everything. It is he who decides how much power will be given to his Prime Minister and Cabinet ministers and even to the legislature. Therefore, the behaviour of each political regime in France comes down to the personality of each President.

Parliamentarians owe their seats to their political parties and constituency links are weak, especially when compared to the UK. However, the regions do have funding and have quite a lot of leeway in deciding how it is allocated.

Even so, if you have a political problem to sort out, it pays to talk to the minister or their advisors (the ministerial 'Cabinet') as their influence is far-reaching, even on highly localised issues.

Industry associations are practically seen as branches of the government and lobbying is a lot less overt than in the US or the UK. This does not mean that industry does not lobby – lobbying is full-on and non-stop in Paris – but it goes on behind closed doors and is highly personalised. Who you know is of primordial importance.

The civil service is a very professional and respected career in France, but it knows little about industry, even if the state plays a big role in directing the economy. The state has significant shareholding in around eighty companies, employing 1.7 million people – including major corporations like Airbus, Orange and Renault. This means that these companies have excellent links with the government and lobbying from the outside is difficult.

The lack of business experience and officials' frequent antipathy towards business makes it difficult to argue on economic terms. The challenge is to persuade politicians and officials why they should be interested in your sector or business. Your first problem will be getting through the door.

The best way is to have a personal contact – reaching out to the ministry 'cold' hardly ever works.

Given all this, when you have finally found the right door to go through, politicians and officials can welcome your input, as they may actually not be very well-informed on what is going on in your business sector. One needs to be patient and build up personal relationships. When you secure this, you will be surprised by how quickly and decisively the government can take action.

However, finding the right door is tricky. Decision-making is opaque and formal stakeholder involvement patchy. You cannot just find a government website detailing who is charge of an issue, whom they are talking to, when they will meet next and register as a stakeholder. A good place to start is to look at the agendas of recent conferences on your subject where a French official was present – get the name and work back to Paris, or ask through a French industry association if your company is a member.

Bureaucracy and bureaucratic delay is pervasive in France. If you have operations in France, the way to tackle this is to patiently build contacts with the local commune, department and region. The dividends come in when you need something in a hurry, or at least on time. Getting approval for a specialist set-up like a new factory paint shop can take eighteen months of official procedures, but if the authorities know you, things can get done in a fraction of the time.

THE UNITED KINGDOM

The UK is similar to France in that the government and the Prime Minister are powerful and the country is centralised.

The officials, or civil service, are apolitical and stay in post whatever happens with politicians and electoral vagaries. Nearly all of them are high-quality career officials. Their biggest problem has been repeated cost cutting and office building closures over the last decade that have stretched resources, from manpower to basic things like finding a spare meeting room and desks for officials – this is something that has not happened to their French counterparts.

You might be surprised by the comment that the UK is highly centralised when you see that it has regional parliaments and mayors, but compared to Germany or Italy their influence is nascent in relation to industry interests. Scotland is the most decentralised country in the UK, with its own legal system and powers in energy and the environment.

The Prime Minister's power and influence is not as specific or as evident as that of the President of France, but nevertheless they are central to how the UK system operates.

The Prime Minister and the ministers have their advisors known inelegantly as SPADs (special political advisors) who help on media and policy matters, but they are relatively few in number. They are important to know and are influential, but they are as fleeting as mayflies compared with the permanent civil servants.

Whatever issues or problems you need to raise with UK politicians, it is nearly always a good idea to make contact and talk with the working officials first. Their support can be extremely helpful if you need to raise your issues at higher levels.

The terminology of titles and positions can be confusing in the UK with titles like the Chancellor of the Duchy of Lancaster (a Cabinet minister), a permanent secretary (a senior-level official) and a parliamentary secretary (a junior minister) that seem to be designed to confuse. The good news is that the UK system is actually the easiest one to navigate. More than once when meeting officials in other European countries I was told that if I wanted to know the details of a European issue I should look on the UK government website, as they did.

All ministries have websites where you can easily find answers to key lobbying questions, such as what is being decided and when, who is making the decision and which industry bodies and activist groups are actively lobbying government.

Members of Parliament (MPs) owe their selection to the local constituency organisation and not just on the central party machinery. This makes MPs much more concerned with local matters than their European counterparts.

As a business you need to take advantage of this local focus. If you have factories in the UK, you should get to know your MP. They can be very helpful in making introductions to decision makers or giving advice. I was always happy when visiting a UK factory to spot a Christmas card sent from the local MP.

SWITZERLAND

Switzerland is not in the EU, but as far as businesses are concerned it is still an important market in Europe. The Swiss may not be around the EU table, but they are active members of other international bodies like the United Nations. So you may end up talking to them about Swiss laws, the complicated subject of how their laws dovetail with EU rules or what they are planning to do at UN level.

Switzerland is highly regionalised into cantons, which have a lot of control over how the rules and regulations apply in each of their territories. The central authorities are relatively weak. However, the centre does regulate and it is ambitious when it does, particularly in the environmental field. Swiss officials have a lot of influence over policy and rule-making.

Swiss politics is insular and it can be difficult to engage with as an outsider but, even so, officials can be approached and it is much easier to be accepted if you have a Swiss colleague with you. It can take some time to build up a good rapport with officials. Probably the biggest problem with the Swiss system is finding out what is going on. Its websites are not informative and often you just have to go to Berne or ask your embassy to find out.

NORWAY

Similarly to Switzerland it is not a member of the EU, but it is part of the single market due to its membership of the European Economic Area (EEA). All the other members of the EEA are also members of the EU apart from Liechtenstein. Norway, however, is not part of the EU Customs Union, so it has formal borders with Sweden.

If you are confused about all these legal niceties, it illustrates how trade relations with close neighbours of the EU can get confusing, as there are layers of agreements and international treaties operating in tandem. For example, Norwegian oil and gas is traded freely into the EU, but its salmon is not, as fisheries are not covered by Norway's agreement in the European Free Trade Area.

Enough of the confusion. Norway is similar to Switzerland in that it is active at UN levels, but it has stronger ties with its Nordic neighbours and is closer to the EU decision-making process. As Norway applies nearly all EU single market legislation, the legal system is relatively simple and its officials are open to meeting outsiders. They are efficient, helpful and are strong supporters of environmental laws.

THE EU PLAYERS

For businesses, probably the most important area of EU rule-making is single market legislation. However, the essential point to note is that it is far from perfect and is a perpetual battleground between protectionists and liberalisers.

This is the political fight you will be getting into. The governments are the most powerful political players. The EU Commission is relatively small, but a central player you need to engage with, being particularly powerful in trade and competition policy and setting the single market agenda. The European parliamentarians are an awkward bunch to deal with, but are important in single market and environmental legislation.

EUROPEAN SINGLE MARKET PREMIER

In national markets, it is a given that there is complete freedom to trade, sell products and provide services throughout the country. Ideally, the European single market would be similarly barrier-free, but its continuing development is a story of bitter struggle.

Trade in products like cars, TVs, computers, aeroplanes, chemicals and beer is now free. Your pets have passports, so they can travel across borders. It is more difficult getting gas and electricity across borders, and it has only been recently that you could use mobile phones across borders without running up outrageous roaming charges.

Progress in services is agonisingly slow. The banking and insurance markets are slowly opening up. You might be able to set up an air tour company in another country, but it is next to impossible to set up a trans-border chain of hair salons or pharmacies.

Agriculture gets oodles of EU money, but when it is regulated at EU level, farmers and governments make sure they are not too troubled by the European Parliament.

As for the defence industry, it is only now making baby steps towards a single market and the defence market remains highly national with little regard to the single market strictures like open competitions.

In single market terms, you could say the most powerful lobbyists are the farmers and soldiers, as they have resisted single market rules for so long.

THE POWER BROKERS OF EUROPE – THE GOVERNMENTS

The real power in the European Union system lies with the

national ministers and their officials. Called the Council, this body is not well-known and its decisions are taken behind closed doors. When decisions are made, the rule of thumb is, if it looks to be popular, the minister will take the credit; if it looks unpopular, the minister can blame 'Brussels' and interfering 'Eurocrats'. This hides the reality that governments hold the whip hand in the EU system.

If you really want to influence how EU laws are made, start with the governments. They are there at the start of the whole process when policies are launched; they are there meeting behind closed doors throughout the debating and decision-making process; and they give the law the final go-ahead.

The hidden nature of the Council allows governments to horse trade (i.e. 'If I say yes to a law (I don't like), you'll let me say no to another'). A classic case of this was Margaret Thatcher reluctantly agreeing to a law for catalytic converters in cars, while the other governments agreed that she could refuse to sign up to the social chapter for workers' rights that she saw as too pro-trade union for her tastes. This decision-making horse trading between completely different policy areas is a difficult aspect of EU law-making to anticipate.

The key to lobbying the Council is to find out which countries are active in discussions. If there is a group that supports your view, go along and see them to make your case. The meetings may be behind closed doors, but the minutes often leak out with helpful footnotes on which countries said what. The ambassadors and national officials going to Council meetings are based in Permanent Representations in Brussels, known as 'PermReps'.

THE CENTRAL PLAYER – THE EUROPEAN COMMISSION

So how about those faceless bogeymen, the Eurocrats in the European Commission? They are well-paid (so that they can be tempted out of their capitals) and are usually capable career officials. At the top, the commissioners, who act much like ministers, have a team of advisors (their 'Cabinet'), much like national ministers.

The Commission is like a super-bureaucracy – having not only the responsibility for preparing and enforcing legislation, but initiating it as well in tandem with European governments. This gives them a central role in decision-making, but they are relatively few in number. Where you find a whole department of officials in a national ministry dealing with an issue, you will find just a couple of Commission officials in Brussels.

Officials at all levels are relatively easy to access and meet. With their limited time and labour resources they are reliant on outsiders to provide information, facts and figures from the real world. A favourite source are consultants – a whole industry has been spawned by the need for Commission officials to find out what is happening in the world when they are preparing policies.

With their central role and longevity in their position, you need to meet the Commission officials working in your area. If they are actively working on policies, you should also find out what their consultants are doing. The consultants can act like a virtual department for Commission people.

The Commission is most powerful in trade policy and competition policy (such as cartel busting and merger approvals), and is central to environmental laws, policing public funding (state aid) and the single market. The latest single market law that has entered some of the public consciousness is one on data protection, where national politicians have not quite decided on whether to take credit for it or to blame Brussels.

As this list of powers covers a lot of what concerns business, getting things right with the Commission is important. It is no surprise that the largest investors in lobbying in Brussels are American and Japanese businesses, as their first step in influencing company-related laws in Europe is the Commission. However, companies in Europe have it easier, as they can go first to their governments before tackling the Commission.

THE AWKWARD SQUAD – THE EUROPEAN PARLIAMENT

The Commission may have been powerful when the great EU projects such as the single market were launched, but it has been superseded by the governments and can get a rough time from the European Parliament.

The European Parliament is nowhere in defence policy, weak to the point of irrelevance in state aid and competition policy and relatively weak in agricultural, energy and transport policy and trade negotiations – but it is powerful in environment and single market legislation.

This definitely gives the Parliament a big chip on its shoulder regarding the Council and the Commission, and a lot of its energy is devoted to competing for power with the other two institutions. Where it has been most successful grabbing power is in single market and environmental legislation.

National blocks of European parliamentarians (members of the European Parliament or MEPs) wielding power is not the norm in the Parliament – that rests with the committees. They work through the details of legislation and present the result for approval by all the MEPs sitting in monthly plenaries in Strasbourg, a French city that borders Germany.

MEPs have a short-term political horizon. EU laws may take three years or more to emerge from the Commission before they are argued over by the Parliament and the governments in about a year or so.

The timings look long when compared to national legislation and the process is definitely complex. The trick is to look at what is due to happen in the next three months and focus on that before taking another three-month bite. MEPs work on a similar timescale. Talk to them about what might be happening in six months, they are not interested.

The numbers of MEPs from each country reflect the

respective population numbers, with Germans being the most numerous. MEPs are a complete mix of characters, but on the whole countries with strong parliamentary systems produce the most active and influential MEPs – the UK, Germany, the Netherlands, Finland, Denmark and Sweden.

The European Parliament elections have to be the least interesting ones in Europe and are met with widespread voter apathy. Voters often take the opportunity to make a protest vote, meaning that many MEPs come from extreme parties on the left and right.

As power in the Parliament is concentrated in the committees, the individual members of these committees working on specific legislation (known as 'rapporteurs') are highly influential. They are much more powerful than their national cousins and, if they play well, as influential as many national ministers.

MEPs, though, have tiny personal offices – a US senator may have fifty people working for them, while an MEP has one or two. When you meet an MEP in their offices and there are more than two of you, you'll have the rather bizarre experience of sitting on a bed. Every office has one in case MEPs decide to work late, but its real role seems to be providing additional seating and filing space.

Busy MEPs are used to a continual stream of people coming in to see them and may get punch drunk. If you are not careful and fail to make a quick impact, the MEP's eyes will glaze over. The usual cause is that arguments and papers that work just fine with officials swiftly bore or confuse the MEP.

MEPs and their assistants hate arguments detailed within sixty-page documents – Brussels is awash with these impenetrable tomes. What the MEP wants is to make political points that can be used and fought for in committee. You have to provide this ammunition.

Ideally, if you make a succinct and compelling case, you'll be asked to put your suggestions down in paper that the MEP can cut and paste into amendments for the committee. Sometimes the cutting and pasting is so enthusiastic that watermarks and other clues to the identity of the lobbyist are transferred to the amendment document. This can be embarrassing all round, so if you are asked to provide 'draft language', make sure it is on a clean document.

However, the MEP you have to work with may not be one of the active ones and this can be very frustrating. In some countries, MEPs have other elected or political jobs in their country that they are much more interested in.

A typical technique to try to get your local MEP involved is to invite them to visit your factory. Painful experience shows that they act like prima donnas and keep you waiting and waiting and then cancel on you. I heard of one German socialist MEP who was proud that he had kept a major German company and employer in his constituency waiting for two years before deigning to visit them.

Of course, there are exceptions to the uninterested and

the no-shows. If many French MEPs are not responsive or reliable, UK and Irish MEPs will generally keep their word if they promise to visit you.

The key to dealing with the European Parliament and MEPs is to work past the prima donnas, the absentees and the lazy, and focus sharply on the MEPs that count – those that are preparing reports and amendments on your issue. Get them sorted and the others will follow.

None of the MEPs like to drag themselves down to Strasbourg – the monthly migration is a pain and an expensive embarrassment – but nevertheless, it is a good idea to go there and meet MEPs in person. They appreciate that you have made the effort to join them in their misery and they will have more time to see you. On the plus side, the food is excellent in Strasbourg.

When you do enter the Parliament building you are free to access MEP offices, but do not be tempted to turn up unannounced at their office doors. Unsurprisingly, they do not like it and your chances of getting a hearing, building up goodwill or forging a rapport is almost non-existent. I heard that one group of lobbyists representing a religion did try this surprise technique by wandering around the parliamentary corridors late at night hoping to accost parliamentarians or their aides. All they achieved was to frighten and annoy the aides, and get themselves a bad reputation into the bargain.

There are other EU institutions – the European Court of Justice, the Committee of the Regions and the Economic and

Social Committee, European Central Bank, and so on – but you are not so likely to have to lobby these bodies.

A EUROPEAN TALE OF HOW A CARROT BECAME A FRUIT

The most important political game in Europe, as far as businesses and organisations are concerned, is creating and deepening the European single market with Europe-wide rules, underpinned by harmonised standards (the process of trying to coalesce existing national laws into a single European rule). I could not resist highlighting the absurdities of what can happen if you try too hard to make everything the same: did you know that carrots are officially a fruit in Europe?

Jam is simple – you spread it on bread and eat it. But give the problem to a set of bureaucrats of defining a 'European' jam and they took fourteen years to decide that it had to be made of fruit. So far, so good then. However, there was consternation all round then when Portugal joined the EU in 1986, as they eat carrot jam. The solution? To classify carrots in EU law as fruit, as no one wanted to reopen the Pandora's box of European jam negotiations.

Ridiculous! But a wonderful example of officials and politicians trying to define things to the nth degree and unintentionally or otherwise blocking new products.

This is a perennial problem in law-making with politicians too tempted to decree prescriptive rules, and a real problem for anyone coming up with new technologies, techniques or services – the rules, unless you are lucky, are never suitable for your type of jam.

When you are lucky, it means that officials have been sensible and the law is not technology-specific. It just sets out what is required, but not how you do it. Thus, a jam could be made of anything.

THE LAST WORD

Stripped to its bones, lobbying is all about persuading the right people at the right time. It is very normal – people are trying to persuade us to do things every day, just as we are doing to them. Whether that is negotiating about taking your turn at the washing up or choosing which brand of cereal you buy in the shops.

Lobbying is not some dark art that can only be practised by the initiated. It is not about coercion, bribery or shouting and screaming to get your way. It is a very human desire to get your point across to people in the best possible way, to persuade them to take your view into account and act on it.

Determination, patience and persistence are invaluable. It takes time to find the right people, and you may have to meet a lot of people before you make progress. Even if you are winning the argument, it may not be apparent at the time.

You may have unwittingly cracked it in what you thought was an inconsequential meeting, and sometimes you have indeed made the killer argument, but it is just taking its time to sink into the system. The political decision-making machine can be frustratingly ponderous when you want a quick result!

Lastly, timing is everything. It is hard to be too early and easy to be too late. The earlier you start, the easier your task is. Ensure that decision makers get to know you and you have more time to build up a network of allies. You are then up and ready; rather than meeting people for the first time when things get more intense, you will already know who your friends and allies are.

People want to be in control of their fate. It is a failure of politicians and governments if they are not responding to the people they represent or govern. Going out lobbying gives you the ability to control or influence your fate. Why leave it to political chance?

ACKNOWLEDGEMENTS

Writing a book about how to go about influencing and persuading politicians has been great fun, but I would never have done it without the support and never-failing encouragement of my wife, who was also a lobbyist in the early part of her career. She gamely read through and commented on the early drafts. She was joined in this endeavour by Harry, my brother, Stuart Rutherford, a specialist in the crop protection industry, and two old colleagues, Jonna Byskata and Pascale Goffin. Apart from their insightful comments and their own stories that enriched this book, they provided that invaluable commodity – encouragement to see it through.

Special mention should also go to Paul Adamson, sometimes described as the 'godfather of Brussels lobbying', who asked me if I would like to write an article about the challenges facing companies lobbying in the era of Brexit for his magazine – when I put pen to paper, the article grew into this book.

My cousin and published author Johnny Roberts provided invaluable advice on the business of getting a book published, as did Jesse Norman MP who was not only generous in his advice, but energetic in inspiring me to see the project through.

Thanks are also due to the team at Biteback Publishing, who not only saw the potential for a business book on lobbying skills, but urged me on throughout the whole writing process.

Lastly, I would like to thank all the politicians, business representatives, association people, journalists and activists whom I have had the pleasure to meet and work with over the years, all of whom have brought so much individual colour and passion to politics.

ABOUT THE AUTHOR

Darcy Nicolle is a career lobbyist who offers support to companies and organisations, helping them get the best for their businesses and employees in the political arena. He has represented multinational corporations, associations and charities in Westminster, Brussels and across Europe at every level, from Presidents and Prime Ministers to parliamentarians and mayors.

Fascinated by politics from an early age, Darcy spent much time with his grandfather, Sir Anthony Kershaw MC MP, watching and sometimes helping him at work. After learning the ropes in Westminster and Whitehall, and realising that the EU institutions were becoming increasingly important for businesspeople, he packed his bags and enrolled at a French university to hone his language skills before embarking on a successful 25-year stint in European and international lobbying.

Darcy lives in Brussels and London with his wife and his beloved cat, Tarquin.